Human Resources Management in India

Emerging Issues and Challenges

Human Resources Management in India

Emerging Issues and Challenges

Edited by

Rabindra Kumar Pradhan
Assistant Professor,
Department of Humanities and Social Sciences,
Indian Institute of Technology (IIT), Kharagpur.

and

Chinmaya Kumar Podder
Executive Director,
Corporate Affairs and Business Development,
Neelachal Ispat Nigam Limited, Bhubaneswar.

New Century Publications
New Delhi, India

NEW CENTURY PUBLICATIONS
4800/24, Bharat Ram Road,
Ansari Road, Daryaganj,
New Delhi - 110 002 (India)

Tel.: 011-2324 7798, 4358 7398, 6539 6605
Fax: 011-4101 7798
E-mail: indiatax@vsnl.com • info@newcenturypublications.com
www.newcenturypublications.com

Editorial office:
LG–7, Aakarshan Bhawan,
4754-57/23, Ansari Road, Daryaganj,
New Delhi - 110 002

Tel.: 011-4356 0919

First Published: **July 2013**

ISBN: **978-81-7708-364-4**

Published by New Century Publications and printed at Salasar Imaging Systems, New Delhi.

Designs: Patch Creative Unit, New Delhi.

PRINTED IN INDIA

SIKSHA 'O' ANUSANDHAN

Deemed to be University

(Declared U/S 3 of the UGC Act, 1956)

Accredited by National Assessment and Accreditation Council (NAAC) with highest Grade 'A'

ISO 9001:2000

Prof. R.P. Mohanty
B.Tech., M.Tech., PGDIP (GM), Ph.D., FNAE, FORSI, FIIIE
Vice-Chancellor

FOREWORD

I am delighted to write this foreword for the book titled **Human Resources Management in India** edited by Dr. Rabindra Kumar Pradhan and Shri Chinmaya Kumar Podder. This book is a remarkable contribution to academia and industry professionals, who might acquire sufficient knowledge by engaging in research and applications of the principles and practices of human resources management. Human resources are the assets of an organization to fulfil its objectives.

While many organizations focus on business strategy and means to achieve growth, quite a good number think about the characteristics of the human resources required to realize their profit, growth and survival objectives. This book presents varied aspects of human resources management.

Formulation and realization of human resources management strategy is a process that has a decisive impact on the organization's results and the sustainability of its value.

There is a positive linkage between the development of human resources/capital and organizational performance. The emphasis on human resources in organizations reflects the view that market value depends less on tangible resources, but more on intangible ones, particularly human resources.

Recruiting and retaining the best employees, however, is only part of the equation. The organization also has to leverage the skills and capabilities of its employees by encouraging individual and organizational learning and creating a supportive environment in which knowledge can be created, shared and applied.

Further, human resources management is one of the big unknowns of research on the determinants of socio-economic development in India. As I know, the majority of empirical and theoretical literature on human resources management suggests the existence of a relationship between social indicators and economic development. In India, I have felt, there is a real dearth of such research. I am confident that this book will generate enthusiastic dynamism among the researchers to undertake serious empirical and quantitative study in the emerging discipline of human resources management.

R.P. Mohanty

About the Book

In recent years, the role of human resources management (HRM) has changed from being reactive to proactive. In the contemporary business scenario, HRM plays a strategic role in an organization's growth and sustainability and is linked with corporate planning, mergers and acquisitions, turnover and rightsizing. Over the years, HRM has asserted the importance of human assets in creating a dynamic and learning organization to successfully compete in the globalized world.

HRM is a process of bringing people and organizations together so that the goals of each other are met. Technological advances, global competition, demographic changes, information revolution and trends towards service society have changed the rules of the game significantly. In such a scenario, organizations with similar set of resources can gain competitive advantage over others only through effective and efficient management of human resources. Presently, HRM is no more an administrative function but a growth-oriented professional function. Human resources managers have to face a number of challenges for managing the modern knowledge-oriented organizations.

The present book contains 17 well-researched papers which provide deep insights into various dimensions of HRM in the Indian context. Authored by academicians and practitioners in the field of HRM, these papers will provide valuable inputs to teachers, students and others interested in the subject.

About the Editors

Dr. Rabindra Kumar Pradhan is Assistant Professor in the Department of Humanities and Social Sciences, IIT Kharagpur. His areas of specialization include social and organizational psychology, industrial psychology, managerial psychology, organizational behaviour and human resources development and management. He has more than 15 years of experience in the field of training, teaching and research in the above fields. He has more than 30 publications in referred journals, news papers, magazines and books. He has participated in many national and international conferences, seminars, symposiums and workshops as paper presenter, chairperson, and invited delegate in India and abroad.

Dr. Pradhan is a member of various professional organizations including International Association of Applied Psychology, International Association of Cross-cultural Psychology, Indian Society for Training and Development, National Academy of Psychology, India, Indian Academy of Applied Psychology, and Indian Science Congress Association.

Shri Chinmaya Kumar Podder is currently Executive Director, Corporate Affairs and Business Development, Neelachal Ispat Nigam Limited (NINL), Bhubaneswar. Prior to joining NINL, he was Deputy General Manager (P&A) of Hindustan Organic Chemicals Limited at Rasayani, Maharashtra. With 35 years of professional experience, he has more than 200 published articles to his credit. In recognition of his contribution to the field of management, he was awarded fellowship of AIMA in 2003, fellowship of NIPM in 2008 and fellowship of ISTD in 2010. He is the only professional in the country to have been conferred with fellowships of AIMA, NIPM and ISTD.

Contents

Contributors

Anupam Ghosh	Department of Management, Birla Institute of Technology, Mesra, Ranchi.
Ansumalini Panda	Assistant Professor in HR, Alard School of Business Management, Pune.
Atri Sengupta	Assistant Professor, Calcutta Business School, Kolkata.
Arun K. Sinha	Senior Vice President, IR and HRD, Jaya Shree Textiles, Howrah, West Bengal.
Birendra Nath Singh	CEO, Dr. Singh and Rao Associates, Visakhapatnam.
Byomakesh Debata	Lecturer, Centurion University of Technology and Management, Bhubaneswar.
Chinmaya Kumar Podder	Executive Director (Corporate Affairs and Business Development), Neelachal Ispat Nigam Limited, India.
Diptendu Simlai	Assistant Professor of Commerce, Dum Dum Motijheel Rabindra Mahavidyalaya, West Bengal State University, Kolkata.
Juthika Sarkar	HR Practitioner, Kolkata.
Lopamudra Hati	Lecturer in HR, Unites School of Business Management, Bhubaneswar.
M. Thenmozhi	Professor, Department of Management Studies, Indian Institute of Technology, Chennai.
Madhusmita Panda	Lecturer in HR, Unites School of Business Management, Bhubaneswar.

Mukesh Kumar Biswas HR Executive, OIL, Assam.

R.N. Misra Head, HR/IR-Legal, Tata Steel, Jameshedpur.

Rabindra Kumar Pradhan Assistant Professor, Department of Humanities and Social Sciences, Indian Institute of Technology, Kharagpur.

Sajeet Pradhan Research Scholar, Department of Humanities and Social Sciences, Indian Institute of Technology, Kharagpur.

Sanchali Sinha Lecturer in HR and OB, Academy of Business Administration, Balasore, Odisha.

Sitanshu Sekhar Das Lecturer, Affinity Business School, Bhubaneswar.

Sumathi, G.N. Research Scholar, Department of Management Studies, Indian Institute of Technology, Chennai.

T.J. Kamalanabhan Professor, Department of Management Studies, Indian Institute of Technology, Chennai.

Uday Kumar Haldar Principal, Swami Vivekananda Institute of Management and Computer Science, Kolkata.

Updesh Kumar Scientist 'F', Defence Institute of Psychological Research, R&D Organization, Ministry of Defence, Delhi.

Vijay Parkash Scientist 'C', Defence Institute of Psychological Research, R&D Organization, Ministry of Defence, Delhi.

Preface

During last three decades, the role of human resources management (HRM) has changed from being reactive to proactive. Today, HRM plays strategic role in an organization's growth and development and is linked with corporate planning, mergers and acquisitions, turnover and rightsizing. Over the years, HRM has asserted the importance of human assets in creating a dynamic, learning organization which not just manufactures products and offer world class services but truly celebrate human potential.

Since people constitute the most significant resource of any organization therefore management of human resources becomes critical for the success of the organization. Human resources management is a dynamic process of bringing people and organizations together so that the goals of each other are met.

With the rapid changes in the business scenario in the recent past, organizations are forced to reorient themselves to meet the new challenges. Technological advances, global competition, demographic changes, information revolution and trends towards service society have changed the rules of the game significantly.

In such a scenario, organizations with similar set of resources can gain competitive advantage only through effective and efficient management of resources. Presently, human resources management is no more an administrative function but a growth-oriented professional function. Human resources managers have to face a number of challenges for managing the modern knowledge-oriented organizations. In the light of these, several new issues have emerged including talent management, outsourcing, performance management, online recruitment, emotional intelligence, team management and impact of information technology and communications.

The premise that people provide organizations with an important source of sustainable competitive advantage is established. The effective management of human capital, as a determinant of organizational performance, is thus accepted. Competition, technology, management and the rise of the new economy, have forced organizations to look for innovative strategies to gain the competitive edge. The role of human resources management in organizations has assumed significance in this context and has been evolving dramatically in recent years. The successful organizations are using human resources as a strategic partner, investing them with far-reaching transformational roles and responsibilities. This activity involves making the function of managing people the most prioritized activity in the organization and integrating all HR policies/programmes within the framework of a company's strategy. Indian organizations are increasingly turning to the HRM techniques to face the emerging challenges posed by liberalization and globalization.

HRM relates to formulation of strategies by business entities concerning selection, training and rewarding of their personnel. The subject has assumed added significance in the wake of liberalization and globalization trends sweeping across the world. In the face of intense competition unleashed by market-oriented reforms, firms are vying with each other to acquire competitive advantage to prosper in business and in many cases to survive in business. Every possible strategy is being applied to achieve the explicit and implicit objectives of the firm. HRM has emerged as an important ingredient of the policy mix to score points over the existing and potential competitors.

Hitherto, corporates in India looked at HRM as a segmented strategy. In the present context of increasing global competition, high customer expectations and emergence of novel business models, time has come when we have to revisit HRM strategy and look at it as a vital input for business. This approach involves aligning of HRM practices with business strategy and harnessing of human capital for business success. Human capital has to be deployed to secure predictable, sustainable and desirable long-term competitive advantage.

Human beings are the heartbeat of an organization. They are the brains trust and think tanks of future strategies. Intangible assets like human capital have to direct tangible and material resources innovatively to fulfil the objectives of any business entity. Vision sharing with employees with adequate empowerment constitutes an essential element of HRM strategy. A system of fair compensation for performance and provision of a good 'work/life balance' and succession planning become important in the context of the 'war for talent', rising salaries and growing levels of attrition, particularly in developing economies like India.

The HRM strategy highlights issues like talent identification, retention and engagement of employees. It has also brought out the need for a gap analysis and measures to fill the gaps in knowledge, talent, productivity and strategy leading to competence building and better position-person fit. A watch has to be kept on demand-supply mismatches and in-house development of multi-skilled personnel to enable companies to diversify, integrate and carry on multiple businesses. These issues call for taking new initiatives in the area of training, imparting skills and empowerment, competence mapping and career development.

With the growing complexity of technology, customer expectations and competitive challenges, there is need for closer industry-academia interaction and more purposeful linkage of theory and practice. Companies have to accord high priority to peoples' development for company's development. This calls for aligning the employees' aspirations with the company's objectives.

The contributors to this volume have covered a wide variety of subjects encompassing important issues like strategic HRM, talent management, garnering competitive advantage through people, career development and succession planning as well as effective recruitment, engagement, retention and competence building strategies. Emphasis has also been laid on keeping employees enthused, empowered and truly engaged.

This book brings together a collection of papers showcasing the best practices and success stories relating to human resources management in Indian organizations. It provides a rich source of information for practitioners and scholars who wish to further their knowledge of HRM practices from an Indian point of view.

Overall, the book could be utilized as a HR tool kit for nurturing and effectively handing human resources by addressing the emerging issues and challenges of employees and employers. The book is a mixture of theory and practice of effective HR. The authors expect that the present book will attract scholars from academics and professionals from industries for its effective use and application.

Acknowledgements

We acknowledge the valuable contribution of many people who are instrumental in the successful completion of this book. This book would not have been possible without the efforts, commitment, and strong devotion of the contributors of this book who tirelessly worked day and night to complete their respective chapters. We sincerely acknowledge their efforts, cooperation and moral and intellectual support during the revision and modification of their works till the final completion.

We place on record our thanks to following scholars for providing encouragement, intellectual guidance, and support: Professor Purnima Mathur, formerly Head of the Department of Humanities and Social Sciences, Indian Institute of Technology, Delhi; Professor Pravash Mishra, formerly Head, Post-graduate Department of Psychology, Utkal University; Professor Abhijit Gangopadhyay, Professor at TISS, Mumbai and XLRI, Jamshedpur; and Professor R.P. Mohanty, VC, SOA University.

We express humble gratitude to our family members,

others colleagues, and friends who directly or indirectly extended their support and encouragement for the completion of this book. Finally, thanks are due to New Century Publications, New Delhi, for accepting the manuscript and co-operating at various stages of the completion of this work.

June 2013

Rabindra Kumar Pradhan
Chinmaya Kumar Podder

1

Current Issues and Future Challenges of HRM

Rabindra Kumar Pradhan

Since people constitute the most significant resource of any organization therefore management of human resources becomes critical for the success of the organization. Human resource management (HRM) is a dynamic process of bringing people and organizations together so that the goals of each other are met.

Importance of HRM in the Changed Scenario

With the rapid changes in the business scenario in the recent past, organizations are forced to reorient themselves to meet the new challenges. Technological advances, global competition, demographic changes, information revolution and trends towards service society have changed the rules of the game significantly.

In such a scenario, organizations with similar set of resources can gain competitive advantage only through effective and efficient management of resources. Presently, human resources management is no more an administrative function but a growth-oriented professional function. Human resources managers have to face a number of challenges for managing the modern knowledge-oriented organizations. In the light of these, several new issues have emerged including talent management, outsourcing, performance management, online recruitment, emotional intelligence, team management and impact of information technology and communications.

The premise that people provide organizations with an important source of sustainable competitive advantage is established. The effective management of human capital as a determinant of organizational performance is thus accepted. Competition, technology, management and the rise of the new economy, has forced organizations to look for innovative strategies to gain the competitive edge. The role of human resource management in organizations has assumed significance in this context and has been evolving dramatically in recent years. The successful organizations are using human resources as a strategic partner, investing them with far-reaching transformational roles and responsibilities. This activity involves making the function of managing people the most prioritized activity in the organization and integrating all HR policies/programmes within the framework of a company's strategy. Indian organizations are increasingly turning to the HRM techniques to face the emerging challenges posed by liberalization and globalization.

What is HRM all About?

HRM relates to formulation of strategies by business entities concerning selection, training and rewarding of their personnel. The subject has assumed added significance in the wake of liberalization and globalization trends sweeping across the world. In the face of intense competition unleashed by market-oriented reforms, firms are vying with each other to acquire competitive advantage to prosper in business and in many cases to survive in business. Every possible strategy is being applied to achieve the explicit and implicit objectives of the firm. HRM has emerged as an important ingredient of the policy mix to score points over the existing and potential competitors.

Hitherto, corporates in India looked at HRM as a segmented strategy. In the present context of increasing global competition, high customer expectations and emergence of novel business models, time has come when we have to revisit HRM strategy and look at it as a vital input for business. This approach involves aligning of HRM practices with business strategy and harnessing of human capital for business success. Human capital has to be deployed to secure predictable, sustainable and desirable long-term competitive advantage.

Human beings are the heartbeat of an organization. They are the brains trust and think tanks of future strategies. Intangible assets like human capital have to direct tangible and material resources innovatively to fulfil the objectives of any business entity. Vision sharing with employees with adequate empowerment constitutes an essential element of HRM strategy. A system of fair compensation for performance and provision of a good 'work-life balance' and succession planning become important in the context of the 'war for talent', rising salaries and growing levels of attrition, particularly in developing economies like India.

The HRM strategy highlights issues like talent identification, retention and engagement of employees. It has also brought out the need for a gap analysis and measures to fill the gaps in knowledge, talent, productivity and strategy leading to competence building and better position-person fit. A watch has to be kept on demand-supply mismatches and in-house development of multi-skilled personnel to enable companies to diversify, integrate and carry on multiple businesses. These issues call for taking new initiatives in the area of training, imparting skills and empowerment, competence mapping and career development.

With the growing complexity of technology, customer expectations and competitive challenges, there is need for closer industry-academia interaction and more purposeful linkage of theory and practice. Companies have to accord high priority to peoples' development for company's development. This calls for aligning the employees' aspirations with the company's objectives.

New Realization about HRM

The concept of HRM emerged during 1980s focusing on the responsible characteristics of successful companies. Later on, many professional bodies and societies came up with ideas that are essentials of effective human resource management. For example, global bodies like American Society for Training and Development (ASTD), Society for Human Resource Management (SHRM) highlighted the important functions of HRM leading to work life balance, quality of life, productivity and willingness to change. In India, many professional bodies like Indian Society for Training and Development (ISTD), National HRD Network (NHRD), and National Institute of Personnel Management (NIPM) have worked seriously to proactively respond to the challenges faced by HR professionals in India. From time to time, both at regional and national level, there are meeting, workshops and seminars to discuss and deliberate on complex issues and challenges of HRM with the changing nature of business environment at national and international level.

People in organizations did not realize for long time that HRM could take them to greater heights of achieving corporate success. It is HRM that can change people and organizations; it is HRM that can make people and organizations to become intelligent and competent; and it is HRM that can motivate people for greater commitment to achieve optimum performance. It is only HRM that can save organizations against all odds. With the passage of time, HRM department has emerged as a strategic partner of all other departments in the affairs of business of today's organizations.

Although, selection, appraisal, reward and development remain the core of all time human resource management for HR professionals, still they struggle with many other issues like work force diversity, gender equity, work place wellbeing, employers branding and talent management. The employee value propositions (EVP) perception has been very instrumental for employees and employers to link personal with professional objectives at work place. In many organizations, there is availability of talents but they struggle with poor performance of employees.

One of the biggest challenges faced by today's organizations is talent retention and talent management. Why organizations struggle with retaining employees even after giving good salary. It points towards the policies and procedures, and provision of organizations to take care of its employees over all development and growth, such as succession planning, career planning and development, employee welfare, quality of life, work life balance. The nature of work also may determine the willingness of a person to continue or discontinue in an organization. Apart from these issues, there are many more that needs to be addressed by HR professionals in the coming years.

HRM Challenges

People and their capabilities in the organizations is increasingly becoming the core to an organizations competitive advantage. The planning and implementation of strategic goals that constitute the human capabilities is taking the centre stage in a business that managers admire about. There is an urgent need to link HR strategy to the overall business strategy of any organization and to pay attention to the burning issues such as performance management, strategic reward systems, and knowledge management systems for strategic advantages and corporate gains.

Strategic HR planning is the process by which an organization ensures that it has the right number of people with the right competencies in the right jobs and at the right cost. Rigorous HR planning links people management to the organization's mission, vision, goals and objectives, as well as to its strategic plan and budgetary resources. It is imperative for organizations to integrate HR planning with business goals right from the start in order to achieve business success.

How to achieve a cost-effective HR that would enhance the organizational revenue is one of the emerging issues of present HR systems. How the organization can maximize its financial performance with minimum investment in its HR is a matter of great concern to all organizations. The initiatives to increase HR competitiveness with fewer expenses come from the top level of the corporate. The issues of achieving HR cost savings are concerned with inefficient processes, difficulty in determining costs, insufficient or ineffective technology, and problems in controlling salary and benefit costs. These are internally generated within HR system of an organization. Other issues are externally generated, such as resistance to change, politics and cost reduction fatigue. Financial compensation along with organizational culture, work environment, and integrity make an employer brand.

Modern organizations are striving to achieve their unique competitive advantage that enables them to become leaders in their industry. In order to achieve true differentiation, companies should develop a responsible and resilient workforce by finding better ways to recruit talent, allocate resources, measure performance and build vital capabilities. HR development and delivery is all about designing and developing sound processes and transparent systems that ensure focused, concerned, committed, and competent workforce in the organization.

These days, organizations are competing with each other in a complex environment. Therefore, an accurate understanding of their goals and the methods for attending those goals is significantly important. The balanced scorecard translates an organization's mission and strategy into a comprehensive set of performance measures that provide a framework for a strategic human resource measurement and management system. The scorecard measures and records organizational performance across four balanced perspectives: financial, customers, internal business processes, and learning and growth. Thus, balance scorecard is an effective parameter of accurate HR audit and measurements to enhance HR effectiveness for organizations.

Corporate social responsibility (CSR) is thought to be an extended human resource management practice that sheds light on the importance of being socially and ethically responsible. If organizations can align their HRD goals with the goals of its socially responsible business dimension, they can survive better in bad times compared to their counterparts in the business world.

2

HRM: Challenges for the Contemporary Business

R.N. Misra

The HR function is increasingly playing a decisive role, delivering expertise that can be leveraged to create greater business value. HR leaders are more often seen as business partners, engaged in strategic decision making. A transformation from a "soft science" concerning "people skills" to that of a "partner" in creating an executive business strategy is underway. HR creates the alignment of HR practices with organizational strategies enabling delivery to promises made to employees, customers, investors and other stakeholders.

As the pace of change increases in global markets, economic uncertainty, and technological advances, leaders must both adapt their organizations and help their employees respond to change. To build both organization capabilities and individual competencies, HR departments, practices, and professionals must be transformed to respond to the challenge of change. It is desirable to understand how the HR transformation is defined and the model to ensure that HR drives business success and avoids the common pitfalls of such efforts. Basically, the HR transformation is a four phase model.

- **Phase 1: Build the Business Case:** HR leaders must know business context and build a case for change.
- **Phase 2: Define the Outcomes**: HR leaders with business leaders define the outcomes of HR transformation as the capabilities of a firm.
- **Phase 3: Redesign HR:** HR leaders redesign their HR

department, reengineer their HR practices, and upgrade their HR professionals.

- **Phase 4: Engage Line Managers and Others:** HR leaders combine with line managers, employees, and advisors to frame and deliver transformation.

HR Transformation model captures both the theory (ideas, rationale, and approaches) and the practices (tools, processes, and actions) for creating a successful HR transformation.

Transformation theory draws from change literatures found in sociology, psychology, anthropology, organization development, systems theory, high-performing teams, and economics. Theory without practice is conjecture and is usually irrelevant. Practice without theory is idiosyncratic and isolated hence the theory and practice need to be combined so that those charged with and affected by HR transformation can make sustainable progress.

A true HR transformation is an integrated, aligned, innovative, and business-focused approach to redefining how HR work is done within an organization so that it helps the organization deliver on promises made to employees, customers, investors, and other stakeholders. This work begins by being very clear about the rationale for doing HR transformation. The rationale for HR transformation is too often from inside the company (say, when a senior business leader complains about HR practices, structure, or people), whereas the rationale should come from outside the company.

Therefore, as the first step to any transformation, HR leaders must clarify the business context. Next, they must be clear about the intended outcomes (or organization capabilities) of the transformation. With outcomes in mind, leaders must align HR to deliver the outcomes by redesigning the HR organization, revamp HR processes, and refocusing HR people. Finally, true HR transformations ensure that long-term initiatives are led by line managers and enabled by HR.

Ultimately, a successful HR transformation increases the value HR adds to the business. This is a simple statement and one that is easy to gloss over, but it reflects an approach to transformation that is not always practiced. The biggest challenge for HR professionals today is to help their respective organizations succeed, and an effective HR transformation will ensure just that.

Phase 1: Business Context

When people understand the why of change they are more likely to accept the what. Hence, an HR transformation should begin with a clear understanding of the business context because the setting in which you do business offers the rationale for the HR transformation you will do. Basic supply-demand logic asserts that if supply is high for any given product or service but demand is zero, then its value is zero. If what we do on the inside does not create value on the outside, in the ability of the company to attract, serve, and retain customers and investors, its value is zero.

HR leaders should not only look at the business strategy but also look *through* the strategy to see and understand the business conditions or external realities that shape it. Understanding and linking HR with these contextual constituents helps HR not just implement the strategy but play a key role in defining it. Ultimately, HR transformation is not about doing HR; it is about building business success.

Phase 2: Outcomes

HR transformation is not a single event—it's a new pattern of thought and behaviour. As discussed above, the rationale for the transformation comes from general business conditions and the ability to increase value to specific stakeholders. Once business leaders acknowledge that HR transformation will help them respond to business challenges, they will inevitably want to know how to measure the impact of the transformation. The HR transformation has two types of outcomes. First, the stakeholder's expectation and second, the capabilities of an organization which is created.

Stakeholder Outcomes: These outcomes should be operationally defined, measured and tracked over time to quantify the progress of HR transformation.

For the stakeholders who matter most, agree upon measures that are reliable, accurate, transparent, and easy to collect for each key stakeholder. As outlined in Table 2.1, the HR team should select the two or three key indicators that will track progress of the transformation.

Table 2.1: Key Indicators

Stakeholders	Possible Measures
Employees	- Greater competence for present and future jobs - Increased retention of talented employees
Leaders and Leadership	- Measure of backup talent (number of qualified people for key jobs) - Ability to "export" top talent to the rest of the company
Customers	- More customer share of targeted customers (share of wallet) - Willingness to recommend firm to others
Regulators	- Give the firm voice in defining regulations - Perceive the firm as one that abides by laws and regulations
Analysts/ Investors	- Higher Price to Earnings (market to book) value - Trust quality of leadership to make the right decisions about strategy, people, customers, and operations
Community	- Manage environment responsibly (reduce carbon footprint) - Gives back to the community (philanthropy) in terms of money and time

Finally, identify how will you collect the data so that you can benchmark where you are now and track where you are going in the future. As you follow these steps, you can begin to see the impact of your HR transformation in terms of outcomes as seen by the stakeholders you serve.

Capabilities as Outcomes: Capabilities shape the way people think about organizations (Table 2.2). These capabilities also become the identity of the firm, the deliverables of HR practices, and the keys to implementing business strategy, and senior leaders must be clear about the two or three "most critical" capabilities the firm must have in order to execute the strategy. Then, they can and should be monitored by measuring and tracking them. There is no magic list of desired or ideal capabilities; however, the following capabilities and their measures seem to be inherent in well-managed firms.

The two to three most critical capabilities represent the outcomes of the HR transformation. They are the deliverables of HR and they lead to the outcomes for each stakeholder. In focusing on capabilities as outcomes, the HR transformation team should do a capability audit where they identify which capabilities are most critical to their organization's future success given business conditions and business strategy. With those prioritized capabilities, scorecards can be created to measure baseline and progress in the critical capabilities. By focusing on both stakeholder and organization capability outcomes, the result of the HR transformation can be defined and tracked.

Phase 3: HR Redesign

The first two phases of HR transformation answer the questions *why* (business context) and *what* (outcomes of HR transformation). The third phase addresses *how* to do the transformation. This phase has three components, each of which is a way of defining what we mean by HR:

1. The HR function or department may need to be redesigned.
2. HR practices may be transformed to be more effectively or more fully aligned, integrated, and innovative.
3. HR professionals may be upgraded to possess the competencies required to do their work.

Table 2.2: Organizational Capabilities

Capability	Description
Leadership	We are good at building leaders that generate confidence in the future.
Strategic Unity	We are good at creating a shared agenda around our strategy.
Customer Connectivity	We are good at fostering enduring relationships of trust with target customers.
Corporate Social Responsibility	We are good at establishing a strong reputation for sustainability, philanthropy, and employability in our industry and community.
Shared Mindset	We are good at ensuring customers and employees have a consistent and positive experience of our firm identity.
Collaboration	We are good at working together across boundaries to ensure leverage and efficiency.
Learning	We are good at generating, generalizing, and implementing ideas with impact.
Innovation	We are good at doing something new in both content and process.
Talent	We are good at attracting, motivating, developing, and retaining talented and committed people.
Speed	We are good at making important changes rapidly.
Efficiency	We are good at reducing the costs of our business practices.
Accountability	We are good at creating and enforcing standards that lead to high performance and execution.

Redesign the HR Department: Transforming an HR department requires building an HR organization that reflects both the business organization and the HR strategy. There are three overriding organization design principles: First, make the HR organization follow the logic and structure of the business organization. Second, make the HR organization follow the flow of any professional service organization. Third, differentiate between transactional and transformational HR work.

Building on these three design principles, the evolving HR organization can have five distinct and at times overlapping sets of responsibilities such as HR service centres, corporate HR, embedded HR, centre of HR expertise and operational executors. These five responsibilities represent channels or ways of doing HR work. The critical issue is to identify the flow of work for each of the five channels in the HR organization, and upgrade each channel to deliver the outcomes from Phase 2. Additionally, awareness of all five channels is helpful in identifying both current and future HR outputs to ensure all outputs are included in your analysis. At times, some try to transform the HR department by focusing on one channel. For example, putting in a new HR information system can increase the efficiency of doing HR administrative work, but this is not a complete HR transformation, unless the other roles are also redesigned.

Revamp HR Practices: People talk about the work of HR as activities, systems, processes, decisions, or initiatives. The work of HR is a set of HR practices because a practice is something that is continually being learned. A practice is also activity within a profession and the concept of best practice defines an activity that delivers an outcome better than some other activity. Transforming HR could mean changing as many as 120 separate HR practices. In *The HR Value Proposition* (Ulrich and Brockbank, 2005), they have synthesized this vast array of HR work into four domains that represent the flows or processes central to organization success.

Flow of People: What happens to the organization's key asset—its people—including how people move in, through, up, and out of the organization. Proper attention to people flow ensures the availability and development of the talent the organization needs to accomplish its strategy.

Flow of Performance Management: What links people to work—the standards and measures, financial and non-financial rewards, and feedback that reflect stakeholder interests. Proper attention to this flow promotes accountability for performance by defining, noting, and rewarding it—and penalizing its absence.

Flow of Information: What information do people need to do their work and how do they get the requisite information. Information can flow up, down, or laterally. It can flow from the outside in or from the inside out. Proper attention to information flow ensures that people know what is happening and why, and can apply themselves to what needs doing to create value.

Flow of Work: Who does work, how work is done, where work is done, and how work is supported through business and operating processes to combine individual efforts into organizational outputs. Proper attention to work flow provides the governance, accountability, and physical setting that ensure high quality results.

Refocus HR People: Ultimately, HR transformation depends on the quality of HR professional s. Given the challenges of understanding the full business context (phase 1), defining important business related outcomes (phase 2), and redesigning the HR department and state-of-the-art HR practices (phase 3), the bar has been raised for HR professionals. What it took to succeed in HR in the past has changed with the emerging challenges. By following the four steps outlined below, leaders can learn to build the competencies of HR professionals.

Step 1: Articulate a Theory and Set a Standard: Successful HR professionals must demonstrate all competencies such as credible activist, operational executor, business ally, organizational designer, culture and change steward and strategy architect within the framework of people and business aligned with relationships, systems and processes and organization capabilities. They must be credible activists and strategic architects.

Step 2: Assess Individuals and Organizations: Establish a methodology for determining how well individual HR professionals do or do not meet the required standards. It is important to receive feedback from a variety of different sources, and consequently, 360 degree feedback processes tend to provide helpful data at a minimal cost. Other assessment methods include self assessments, psychometric testing, intense behavioural based assessments, and job performance assessments.

Step 3: Invest in Talent Improvement: After a gap has been identified—both for each individual and for the department as a whole—the next step is investment. Investing in HR professionals means allocating time and resources to upgrading their skills through job experience, training experience and life experience.

Step 4: Follow up and Track Competence: The final step in any talent improvement model is measuring and following up. Measurement means tracking the quality of the HR professionals and of the investments to develop the HR professionals. Having a baseline of HR performance and then regularly benchmarking against that baseline allows HR leaders to present progress to their business leaders. Actively measuring the impact of investments in HR people against the stated outcomes of the alignment and create continued emphasis on the transformation will ensure right results.

Phase 4: Engage Line Managers and Others

A successful process of HR transformation involves the right people at the right time in the right way. We call this phase 4, but it is a critical feature of all phases. The importance of involvement in successful change management is well established. We know from decades of social-psychological research that people are more likely to be committed to activities or decisions in which they are involved. Four groups of stakeholders should be involved with the HR transformation: HR, line managers, customers and investors, and external consultants.

HR Leaders and Professionals: HR's role is to design the process and enable the implementation of the transformation.

HR transformation depends on the quality of HR professionals and their relationships with line managers. Four roles are important to this process: the chief HR officer (CHRO), the HR leadership team, the head of HR for HR, and HR professionals.

Line Managers: Line Managers must make sure the transformation aligns to business goals and work with HR to implement the transformation. Line managers are ultimately accountable for ensuring that the organization has the right talent and right organization in place to deliver on expectations to customers, shareholders, and communities. They have the responsibility to provide a clear business focus for the transformation, to ensure that the transformation team has access to both external and internal information, to ensure that the right people are involved in the transformation process, and to require clear and measurable results from the transformation.

External Customers and Investors: HR Leaders and Line Manager must seek the guidance of external customers and investors throughout the HR transformation to ensure relevance. Often HR transformation comes from and is driven by an internal logic. Frequently logic, language, and practices of HR focus on employees' needs. As an alternative, as stated above, HR must be built from the outside in and should focus on its impact on external stakeholders who matter to the company.

Consultants and Advisers: Those who have successfully engaged external consultants hire them with the specific request to offer frameworks and insights developed and proven over time, and point out potholes that others have stumbled into. If focused, our experience suggests that consultants can add value in a number of specific ways and at a number of specific points in the process.

Conclusion

As depicted above, a true HR transformation is an

integrated, aligned, innovative, and business-focused approach to redefining how HR work is done within an organization so that it helps the organization deliver on promises made to customers, investors, and other stakeholders. Ultimately, a successful HR transformation increases the value HR adds to the business. As leaders complete the four phases of HR Transformation, HR professionals become full partners in helping a business move forward. HR can help organizations get the maximum value from their people and their organization while ensuring they treat them as individuals with unique needs, aspirations, and dreams.

References

Ulrich, D. and Brockbank, W. (2005), *The HR Value Proposition.* Harvard Business School.

Ulrich, D., Allen, J., Brockbank, W., Younger, J. and Nyman, M. (2009), *HR Transformation: Building Human Resources from the Outside,* McGraw Hill.

3

Building Young Leadership

Uday Kumar Haldar and Juthika Sarkar

"Education is the manifestation of the perfection already in man" –*Swami Vivekananda*

Business Environment

A business house runs broadly under general environment, task environment, and competitive environment, and with the cooperation of business associates. Various other environments in which a business operates are social, cultural, economic, technological, political, and international environments. All these environments are interdependent. It is essential to conform to certain societal and cultural norms, consider the national economic system at macro level and decide upon the pricing mechanism at micro level. Competitors, existing or emerging, their strategies, market, reputation, product costs, etc. sway and influence the business tactics of an organisation.

Environment comprises of forces or institutions which are outside the business organization, but substantially affect its performance. Business environment affects business management; particularly human resource management. Business environment must be subjected to analysis on different criteria.

For convenience of analysis, environment may be classified on different criteria such as space, time, forces, and factors.

- **Space:** It encompasses the local, regional, national, and international environment.
- **Time:** It speaks about the past, present, and future

environment.

- **Forces**: It includes the market as well as the non-market environment.
- **Factors:** It spreads over economic and non-economic environment.

The environmental factors may be exogenous or endogenous. Moreover, the factors are interrelated, interactive, and interdependent. A business needs to adapt to the environment and adopt to suitable human resource management initiatives in addition to strategic management drives. The adaptation to a particular environment, obviously, also needs consideration of space, time, forces, and factors. Usually, it becomes a little difficult for these companies to keep a tab on all these factors. So, in order to overcome this hassle, questionnaires are framed for an organization to go through for framing any strategy.

Changes in Business Environment

Following liberalization and globalization, the socio-cultural environment, both economic and non-economic environment or domain, educational, politico-legal environment, technological environment, international environment, task environment are changing. Regulating bodies and agencies are imposing various rules to be followed. Added to these social responsibilities of business houses are impacting the businesses.

Few examples of some businesses like retail industry, aviation industry, information technology sector, outsourcing services, and academia are highlighted which happened due to the recession.

Till the world-wide recession, retailers like *Shopper's Stop* was busy in chasing headhunters to find candidates 'willing to join' them. Later, the company decided to be very selective in filling up new vacancies and to recruit only when new stores came up. It was evident that the tables had turned. Future Group said that companies owning large retail chains like

Pantaloon and Big Bazzar had cut people cost by 1 percent by linking salaries with performance and further emphasized that, 'human capability is infinite and multi-tasking is the order of the day'.

In the aviation sector, Jet Airways laid off 800 employees and announced a further lay-off of 1,150 employees. However, the laid off employees were reinstated within 24 hours after public and political outcry. The company was reeling under pressure and was experimenting. In the same sector, Kingfisher Airlines slashed the salaries of the co-pilots by 90 percent.

Wipro Technologies had put 4-5 percent employees under scanner for non-performance though it said that, 'this is a regular annual exercise'. Bangalore-based IT service provider MphasiS (part of EDS) reduced hiring plans by almost 50 percent. It had earlier announced that it would recruit 8,000 people but later, the company planned to recruit only 4,000 people. Teamlease, the largest staffing solution company of India, were earlier recruiting people without much emphasis on job specification. Now it has changed its recruitment strategy. It is obvious that we have moved from 'plenty' to 'paltry'.

All the above facts are posing threats and challenges to the organisations, who are now finding ways and means 'to get more from people', encouraging working in teams for which they are looking for leaders capable to unite, motivate, drive, and produce results.

In view of the changing business scenario, growing complexities, acute competitions, government policies the model of leadership is also changing. Humility is essentially required to be an effective leader. At present a person needs to be creative. Though a leader must be tenacious; what is required at present is that he has to execute everything.

In order to cope with the paradigms the leaders need to adopt few styles that suit the specific situations. Table 3.1 brings out the leadership requirements that have emerged.

Leadership Styles

Managers are organisational leaders. They are required to bring into play variety of leadership styles in order to get the jobs done and to achieve the organisational goals. The contemporary leadership styles are transactional, transformational, charismatic leadership, value based leadership, spiritual and servant leadership, boundary spanning and team leadership, and 'Level 5' leadership.

Table 3.1: Emerging Leadership Requirements

Conventional	Emerging
Humility	Creativity
Tenacity	Execution is everything
Ability to go against flow	Vision and innovation
Facilitate	Planned abandonment
Negotiate	Creates simultaneously
Articulate	Create contents
Understand business issues	Work with more competent people
Detachment/ Egolessness	Ability to engage
Tough Expectations	Recognize, create and address larger constituents
Personal discipline	Balanced EQ/IQ
Scalability	Network
Ability to take difficult decisions with speed	Ability to seek help

Source: www.cii-iq.in

Transformational leaders concentrate on changes, innovations, apply discretion, and possess entrepreneurial zeal. This brand of leadership is a behavioural process capable of being learned and managed. Transformational themes include recognition of the need to change, creating a new vision, and institutionalizing the change. These leaders need *Sattva* and *Rajas* gunas for success. Charismatic leaders generate loyalty, dedication, trust, commitment, and emotional involvement; distil complex ideas into simple messages to stimulate the followers. Value based leaders can foresee the direction and speed of changes; rely heavily on their voluntary relationship with work and workforce. They do not prefer to use authority and exercise power for task accomplishment, but followers do what is required of them.

Spiritual leadership possess inner beauties, lay emphasis on vision, altruistic or selfless love, hope, faith, and contributes to effective performances. Servant leaders treat their key roles as developer, enabler and supporter of the team members, achieve power on the basis of their values and ideals; treat their key roles as those of developing, enabling and supporting their team members, helping them fully develop their potential and deliver their best.

Boundary spanning leaders perform representative where their loyalties remain entirely to the group and linking-pin functions to interact with two or more groups when their loyalties remain with both groups.

A 'Level 5 Leader' is an executive who builds enduring greatness through a paradoxical combination of personal humility plus professional will.

Emotional Intelligence Base of Leadership Styles

Some leaders are using coercive style, authoritative style, affinitive style, democratic style, pace setting style, and coaching style. They do so based on emotional intelligence bases. Table 3.2 highlights the emotional intelligence bases against the leadership styles.

Leaders must have communication skills including adequate skills of emphatic listening. Leaders should neither be passive nor aggressive; rather they need to be assertive. They must possess relevant technical competency and skills of setting goals objectively. The ten discrete skills for empathetic listening identified by Marisue (1986) are—attending, reiterating; reflecting, interpreting, synthesizing, probing, providing feedback, supporting, verifying perception, and being quite.

Table 3.2: Emotional Intelligence Bases against Leadership Styles

Leadership Styles	Emotional Intelligence Base
Coercive style	Desire to achieve, initiative, self-control
Authoritative style	Self-confidence, empathy, change catalyst
Affiliative style	Empathy, building relations, communication
Democratic style	Collaboration; team leadership; communication
Pace setting style	Conscientiousness, drive to achieve, initiative
Coaching style	Developing others, empathy, self-awareness

Furthermore, in order to develop the listening skills one has to be careful about the following:

1. Developing the desire to be directed by others, the team members, rather than to project one's own feelings, thoughts, and ideas onto the others.
2. Sacrificing behaviour to protect self—unless this is done, it would be difficult to focus and honour other persons' views.
3. Respecting others experience, credentials, thoughts, viewpoints, etc.
4. Interpreting the importance of the roles, perspectives, or responsibilities of others rather than assuming they are the same as one's own.
5. Cultivating the habit to listen as a receiver, but not as a critic, and the desire to understand other persons; their strengths and weaknesses for their constructive uses.

Apart from the basic skills, leaders need some more vital skills generally termed as advanced skills which are time management, delegation, managing conflict, persuasiveness, negotiation and problem solving skills.

Time Management

Leaders often suffer from stress due to work pressure. Gradually, the pressure leads burnt out stress syndrome and then to health problems. Thus, managing time is an essential need of a leader. As a leader you must be performing very urgent as well very important activities in addition to many normal activities. You should entrust majority of the activities to your junior colleagues. You should not be afraid thinking that the junior may keep aside some important work and delay execution of something urgent.

The team leader must assess and consider the strengths and weaknesses, regularity and sincerity of the members. You should monitor but desist yourself from close supervision. Leaders should prepare an exhaustive list of activities they are performing, classify the activities based on urgency (urgent and very urgent) and importance (important and very important). You can do the very urgent work yourself. Assign important tasks to the sincere junior. The rest of the activities you can divert to juniors.

Certain steps are suggested that may enable you to manage time (Haldar 2009).

Step 1: First classify the activities based on urgency (urgent and very urgent) and importance (important and very important).

Step 2: Then prepare a matrix and place the activities in the respective cells. Prepare a matrix as I am showing you.

Step 3: After segregating the activities, concentrate only on activities belonging to the category VI-VU, that is, very important and very urgent.

Step 4: Assign the VI-U tasks to a junior who is regular in his work.

Step 5: Delegate the I-VU tasks to the sincere junior.

Step 6: Detail staff members to carry out the I-U tasks. Develop a system and procedure, and issue work instructions for these tasks. Assign the task of monitoring to the junior managers.

Step 7: Oversee the system occasionally.

Delegation

Delegation is transferring authority from one organizational level to another lower level, assigning authority for work to junior colleagues allowing him to make decisions that enable to manage time. Delegation is basically a four-step process—allocation of duties to subordinate, delegation of authority, assignment of responsibility, and creation of accountability. In fact, on receiving authority responsibility develops from within.

The principal purposes of delegation are developing juniors, inculcating leadership skills and enable them to make decisions with the ultimate objective to fill in the leadership pipeline. The juniors can consider all inputs meticulously and the quality of decision improves. It is needless to mention that subordinates get stimulation, energy, which in turn enhances their commitment. A junior, on receiving authority feels him/her responsible and boldly accepts the accountability. Furthermore, the relationship between the dyads, the senior who has delegated and the junior who has received the authority, enhances. In addition, delegation frees up the senior when he can utilize the time in doing creative activities.

Determinants of Delegation: The organizational culture is a powerful influencer of managers' delegation. Tolerance for risk, support for employees, and high degree of autonomy, system of working, extent of decentralization, are few organizational characteristics in which managers feel more comfortable to delegate. But, in risk-aversive situation, non-supportive and high control culture, managers hesitate to delegate. Also juniors hesitate to accept the higher responsibilities.

Managing Conflict

Conflict, intra-personal or interpersonal, is part and parcel of organizational life. Conflict does not develop all of a sudden. When one individual perceives that the other individual is dynamic and making some conscious effort to frustrate him, then the conflict episode begins.

To manage the conflict, the leader may impose a solution, choose diffusion strategy, smooth out the same, or appeal to the team goal.

While imposing a solution the leader should study the antecedent conditions, finalize a solution, and impose on the conflicting members. The conflict diffusion strategy attempts to keep the conflict in abeyance. The emotions of both the parties are allowed to precipitate down. The smoothing has been found to be successful where the conflicting members have some similarities. In this technique the leader may highlight similarities between the members. This enables both the parties to realize that they are not basically much apart from each other in regards to their viewpoints, perception and psychological bases. Appealing to the organisational goal pacify the conflicting parties.

Different authors have given different taxonomies like conflict avoidance strategy, conflict diffusion strategy, conflict containment strategy, and conflict confrontation strategy. A leader needs skill to identify the strategy suitable in a particular situation. During handling conflicts one must also keep in mind certain points. Welcome differences—divergent views of members can always be there. Find something positive in the every divergent view and bring it to limelight. React assertively and positively, use empathy and positive feedback, confront problems, and negotiate solutions together.

Persuasiveness

Persuasiveness refers to conscious manipulation mainly through face-to-face communication to induce and stimulate others to take action that helps the first party to achieve a goal. Persuasion means influencing but yet differs from authority and power. Persuasion does not encroach in other's area of interest as it preserves his freedom. At times, when authority won't work, persuasion often can. Persuasion needs credibility, logical reasoning, and emotional support.

Negotiation

Negotiation implies compromise, conciliation, and cooperation. It is the process in which two parties exchange goods or services or ideas leading to a contractual agreement. Negotiation occurs when someone else has what you want and you are prepared to bargain for it and vice versa (Kindersley, 2000). Kindersley emphasizes utmost need of creating a right atmosphere to make the negotiation effective. A negotiation process might have three possible outcomes: (a) sudden death due to break down, (b) an acceptable compromise, and (c) achieving ideal outcome for which the negotiation had been organized. Kindersley (2000) elucidates the various steps of the above outcomes.

Even if the opening position is carefully planned the negotiation can follow planned as well as unplanned route. If the negotiation follows the planned route an ideal outcome is achieved. Negotiation follows an unplanned route then it may lead to a longwinded route wasting time. It can even move through a dangerous route with lot of arguments ending with a breakdown of the negotiation. On the other hand in case of longwinded route wastes time but may lead to finding an acceptable compromise and achieving an ideal outcome. The duration should not exceed two hours without a break. Negotiation skill can be learnt and a skill that get sharpened over years.

Problem Solving

Problem solving emphasizes finding out a mutually satisfactory solution. The solution must reconcile and integrate the needs of both parties who work together. The most critical ingredients in successful problem solving as summarized by Alderfer are:

1. Definition of the problem should be a joint effort based on shared fact-findings rather than on the biased perceptions of the individual groups.
2. Problems should be specific and not abstract.
3. Points of initial agreement and also the differences in the goals and benefits of both the parties should be identified.
4. Discussion between the groups should consist of specific

but non-evaluative comments. Any question may be asked for clarification of information but not to humiliate the opponent.

5. Groups should work together in developing alternative solutions. Each group may present a range of solutions.
6. Solutions should be evaluated "objectively" in terms of "quality" and "acceptability". In some cases the solution may maximize joint benefits but favour one party. To make the solution equitable some was to be found to provide special benefits to the other party.

All agreements on separate issues to be considered tentatively until all the issues are dealt with. The issues may be inter-related.

Technical Competency

Leaders need variety of competencies to achieve the goals, of which technical competency is a unique one. This competency helps them in direct interactions, such communicating and building personal network and relationships with others. In fact, leadership competency comprises skills and behaviours concerned with building teams and getting results through the team members. The competencies that relate to analyzing issues, generating alternatives, selecting the best, considering financial positions, thinking strategically, and making decisions fall in the category of business skills. Technical competencies refer to knowledge about system, processes, procedures or methods, and techniques for conducting a specialized activity as done by engineers, doctors, musicians, players, accounts, and other professional. This competency is also the ability to select and use equipment, a procedure, standing instructions, technique and knowledge.

Goal Setting

Setting goals for self, a team member, or the team as a whole needs experience, maturity and pragmatism. If the goals are specific and the roles are clear and unambiguous, members can perform better. Specific goals lead higher performance. Each goal must be split into its elements and time be allotted. Completion of each element must be closely monitored. Consider the objective of productivity enhancement. To achieve this objective you are first required to consider the product range and logically segregate that. Consider a particular group of products, estimate the level to which you can enhance the output or reduce the resources required. You have to take into account all constraints you might encounter. The time you estimate to achieve an element or work package must be lesser than that of the objective. This will enable you to initiate action if any element takes more time. In order to monitor the progress you have to set the goal in measurable terms.

Assertiveness

Leaders should be assertive; neither be passive nor aggressive. Assertiveness is social boldness—a dominant determinant of performance—in any work sphere, manufacturing or service sector. Assertiveness is essentially required by any human being to achieve success, irrespective of the nature of engagement. An assertive person can execute his duties efficiently and effectively. The level of assertiveness greatly affects the performance of any individual and is a dominant factor responsible for the successful accomplishment of the job. Assertive employees participate more broadly, take on greater responsibilities, express their ideas and interact with greater varieties of people, solve problems objectively, find solutions, and implement them with little or no resistance.

Assertive persons get the willing support of their team-mates and colleagues. They can manage conflict effectively. They do not avoid but accommodate, do not compromise but collaborate with others. Assertiveness is an employee's personal quality significantly required in the area of quality management. Assertiveness is a positive and constructive way of relating to other people respecting their needs, wants, and rights, as well as one's own needs, wants, and rights. Assertiveness is an antidote to fear, shyness, passivity, and even anger, and so there is an astonishingly wide range of situations in which assertiveness is appropriate. (Schimmel, 1976) He suggests several kinds of assertive behaviours. Assertive persons exhibit certain characteristics.

Characteristics of Assertive Persons

Some of the characteristics demonstrated by assertive persons are as follows:

1. Be specific, honest and straightforward.
2. Buy time.
3. Care over use of language.
4. Be aware of the way you say things.
5. Use appropriate body language, which confirms the verbal message.
6. Be prepared to withdraw to re-group.
7. Criticize the task NOT the person.
8. Learn to say "No" (in demanding situation) and mean it.
9. Remember that you have rights and exercise that.
10. Be prepared to listen.
11. Be prepared to negotiatc if appropriate.
12. Learn to agree to disagree.
13. Stick to the point.
14. Play the broken record whenever needed.
15. Deflect criticism.
16. Acknowledge own mistakes.
17. Be well prepared.

Assertive Responses

Assertive persons talk and respond in such a way that leads win-win situation. Ten types of assertive responses are as follows:

1. Assertive talk: Do not let others take advantage of you. Insist upon being treated with fairness and justice. Examples: "I was here first," "I'd like more coffee please.,"

"Excuse me, but I have another appointment," "please turn down the radio." or "This steak is well-done and I ordered it medium-rare."

2. Feeling talk: Express your likes and dislikes spontaneously. Be frank about your feelings. Do not bottle emotions. Answer questions honestly. Example: "What a marvelous shirt!" "I'm tired as hell," "Since you asked, I would much prefer you in another type of outfit."
3. Greeting talk: Be outgoing and friendly with people whom you would like to know better. Do not avoid people because of shyness, because you do not know what to say. Smile brightly at people. Look and sound pleased to see them. Examples: "Hi, how are you?" "Hello, I haven't seen you in months." "What are you doing with yourself these days?" How do you like working at so and so .....?" "Taking any good courses" "What's been happening with so and so?"
4. Disagreeing passively and actively: When you disagree with someone do not feign agreement for the sake of "keeping the peace" by smiling, nodding, or paying close attention. Change the topic. Look away. Disagree actively and emotionally when you are sure of your ground.
5. Asking why: When you are asked to do something that does not sound reasonable or enjoyable by a person in power or authority, ask why you should do it. You are an adult and should not accept authority alone. Request explanations from teachers, relatives and other authority figures that are convincing. Have it understood that you will live up to voluntary commitments and be open to reasonable suggestions, but that you are not to be ordered about at anyone's whim.
6. Talking about self: When you have done something worthwhile or interesting, let others know about it. Let people know how you feel about things. Relate your experiences. Do not monopolize conversations, but do not be afraid to bring them around to yourself when it is

appropriate.

7. Agreeing with compliments: Do not depreciate yourself or become flustered when someone compliments you with sincerity. At the very least, offer an equally sincere "Thank you." Or reward one who compliments by saying, "That's an awfully nice thing to say. I appreciate it." In other words, extend compliments. For example: If someone says, "What a beautiful sweater!" respond, "Isn't it a lovely colour? I had a hard time finding it."
8. Avoiding trying to justify opinions: Be reasonable in discussions, but when someone goes out of his way to dominate a social interaction by taking issue with any comments you offer, say something like, "Are you always so disagreeable?" or "you seem to have a great deal invested in being right regardless of what you say, don't you?"
9. Looking people in the eye: Do not avoid the gaze of others. When you argue, express an opinion, or greet a person, look him or her directly in the eye.
10. Saying no: When a request is unreasonable, when you feel your rights are being denied, or when you feel you are being taken for granted, say "No" and persist in your no. Offer other suggestions so that the request might be met. Offer an explanation but don't explain to the point of defensiveness. Examples: "No. I need to study right now." "I realize that this is an important cause and I certainly wish you the best of luck in getting volunteers, but I must say no."

It is imperative to elucidate the way assertive people converse using selective words.

Example of Assertive Words

Choose assertive words carefully.

Example 1: Use factual descriptions, do not offer verdict Compare the following:

"This is a sloppy work, carelessly done." (Boss is

Aggressive)

"The pages (say, 7, 10, 24, 26...) of this Draft HR Manual are not in order. Please review and submit." (Now he is Assertive)

Example: Avoid exaggerations: Compare the following:

"You are never coming on time in the HR planning meeting!" (The HR manager is Aggressive)

"(Looking at the record of attendance) the HR manager said, in the last meeting also you were late by more than one hour. You are 45 minutes late today. Please ensure timely arrival." (Now he is Assertive)

Use "I" to the extent possible and not "You".

Organisations need to conduct training programmes to build up basic skills of leaders and develop advance skills in addition to the most important assertive communication.

Organisations need to identify talents and acquire, nurture, and retain them to gain competitive advantages and achieve distinctive competence.

A talented employee with high potential can make a significant difference to the current and future performance of the organization.

Talent management is a conscious, deliberate approach to attract, develop and retain people with the aptitude and abilities to meet current and future organizational needs.

Talent Management Continuum

The gamut of talent management is widespread. In short, talent management continuum encompasses:

1. Acquiring talent: manpower planning and recruitment.
2. Retaining talent: induction and placement.
3. Nurturing talent: performance management system.
4. Multiplying talent: development system.
5. Developing talent: multi-source feedback.
6. Advancing talent: potential appraisal and career system.
7. Recognizing talent: reward system.
8. Promoting talent: compensation management.

9. Networking talent: separation and beyond.
10. Engaging talent: developing workers and subordinate staff.

Activities to manage talents includes influencing, priority fixing (time management), integrity verification, attitude survey, problem-solving, watching organizational culture, observing organizational climate, creating positive change, etc.

Know Your People

A leader should know the followers as a 'mother knows her baby'. The essentials of knowing the followers are:

1. Making out their organizational role stress.
2. Identifying their level of motivation.
3. Discovering their personality trait.
4. Measuring their assertiveness.
5. Determining their level of job satisfaction (use multi-faceted scale).

- Pay: Pay and remuneration,
- Promotion: Promotion opportunities,
- Supervision: Immediate supervisor,
- Fringe benefits: Monetary and non-monetary fringe benefits,
- Contingent rewards: Appreciation, recognition, and rewards for good work,
- Operating procedure: Operating policies and procedures,
- Co-workers: People you work with,
- Nature of work: Job and tasks themselves, and
- Communication: Communication within the organization.

Creativity and Innovation

Peoples are imaginative, inventive, risk-takers and challengers. But, these dimensions differ in the magnitude. The value of what people produce depends on their originality and creativity. You may recall that, 'Winners do not do different things; they do things differently'. Creativity is the ability to solve problems that are worth solving. It is the ability to create and use knowledge to solve a specific problem, subject-specific and the 'meta-knowledge' of how to solve a specific class of problems. Creativity is the bringing into being of something that did not exist before, either as a product, a process or a thought. A person needs opportunity to be creative and apply creativity. Creativity drives the generation of ideas, and organisations need new ideas constantly.

Fostering Team Creativity

Large organizations today encourage people to work in teams, and strive to foster creativity in the teams. They take up an already existing team and try to make the team more creative than it would otherwise tend to be. Brainstorming is the tool that is mostly used to foster creativity leading to problem–solving. Brainstorming is a structured approach to creativity with the freewheeling problem-solving approach. Lateral thinking is a heuristic for solving problems looking at the problem from many angles instead of remaining stuck with one only. Creative thinking, an instinctive talent a person possesses and set of skills, can be learned, developed, and utilized in the work area. Brainstorming is a systematic technique used for changing concepts and perceptions, exploring multiple possibilities and approaches and to generate new ones. Not all people are creative though creativity can be fostered.

A leader has to turn individuals into team players, make the teams effective, shaping team behaviour, maintain a mature team, manage dysfunctional teams and many such works. Therefore, leaders need to foster team creativity, gain and utilize collective wisdom.

Phases of Creativity

Creativity, the instinctive talent of a person, develops in phases like preparation, immersion, incubation, illumination, evaluation, and application. (Goman, 2004)

- Preparation means doing the groundwork like information

gathering, data collection, and opinion survey etc. whichever one feels relevant to the project or assignment undertaken.

- Immersion—this is the stage when one should be totally absorbed in the situation or problem and concentration on all the appropriate and significant facts, figures, concerns, and angles. Opinions are the connotations of this stage.
- Incubation—when a man takes rest, his mind becomes subconscious which is a far more fertile ground for creativity and has no judgmental or censoring elements when ideas are free to recombine in unique ways, invade in novel ways.
- Illumination—in subconscious mind you may suddenly get the solution. The sudden appearance of the answer to your problem in the form of an image, an insight, a thought breaks through to conscious awareness and comes to you.
- Evaluation—at this stage one has to test the practicability of the idea in reality considering all possible consequences.
- Application—this is the final phase when the creativity is translated into an innovative reality, tangibility, value, usefulness, and meaningfulness. A creative workgroup or team differentiates itself from others based on its hallmark.

It is essential to take a momentary look of various facets f team working like collective intelligence, wisdom, and consciousness.

Collective Intelligence, Wisdom, and Consciousness

The hallmark of a creative group is the extent of to which a prolific flow of ideas can take place in a group. (Belbin, 1981) Collective intelligence, collective wisdom, and collective consciousness are all different. (Macdonald, 2008) Collective intelligence refers to the external, methodological and operational aspects of social organizations to raise their intelligence as a whole. The astounding and surprising effects of collective intelligence are appearing as a topic-of-interest world wide, in the natural sciences as well as the social sciences. Collective wisdom is the access to and the manifestation and demonstration of wisdom, at a collective level. Collective consciousness is the sense that each member of a team, each participant of a brainstorming session has about the consciousness of the team. It is a space one can access at anytime to sense what the context is and what is likely to emerge. Organisations need to arrange workshop to instil creativity and derive benefits from the collective intelligence, wisdom, and consciousness.

Empowerment

Senior managers must delegate considering capabilities of juniors as discussed earlier. Furthermore, they need to empower enabling the juniors to apply discretion, which obviously must have certain boundary. The leader must specify the range. Preferably all the parameters should be categorized, and then category-wise range specified. Subordinate must be encouraged and allowed to participate and develop. It may not be possible to assess at start how much empowerment will be necessary for task accomplishment. But the person who will be held accountable must have authority. Therefore, the subordinate may be cautiously allowed to participate while taking decision on how much authority will be required. Empowerment restores organisational belongings and involvement, and reduces possibility of attrition.

Accountability

In organization often the roles of managers remain undefined resulting overlaps. The overlap allows—-indeed actively encourages—each individual or business unit to "pass the buck" to the others. Ultimately, in the severely non-aligned system, no one is accountable for anything. In this event, the principle of accountability breaks down completely. Organizational failure is the only possible outcome. Business run on true principles of accountability in addition to transparency, equity, integrity and responsibility can make a difference that could give enormous pride to executives and provide the true incentive for driving the corporations.

The synonyms of accountability are answerability and answerableness. Accountability refers to obligation of an individual, firm, or institution to account for its activities, accept responsibility for them, and to disclose the results in a transparent manner. It also includes the responsibility for money or other entrusted property. Young managers must be held accountable for his benefit and organisational benefit.

Training and Development Interventions

Organisations can create a framework such that managers and staff at all levels in the business have training and development opportunities which enhance their career development as well as the business aims. Without a carefully formulated strategy, the training and development activities will not deliver the return on investment which organisations are looking for.

The interventions should be typically designed to save investment of money by ensuring that all training and development interventions are precisely targeted for productive business outcomes. All people need leadership skills whatever be the managerial level. However, organisations need to focus sharper attention onto young leaders as some of them are likely to occupy the top management hierarchy as successors to departing leaders. As we should make the doll when the clay is soft, we need to shape the behaviours of young leaders. But young professionals, too, must simultaneously strive hard to improve their emotional quotient as a powerful communicative societal tool.

Leadership development has emerged as a vital organisational need. Many organisations have developed leadership development centres. Leadership development at Infosys Technologies is worth mentionable.

A leadership development model (Haldar, 2010) as appendix to this piece of writing is relevant and may be referred to while designing the raining curriculum on leadership.

Leadership Development at Infosys Technologies

1. Vision behind Infosys Leadership Programme: The vision of Infosys is to create an organisation that is 'built to last', and has the agility and liveliness to manage ambiguity and uncertainty under all circumstances. N.R. Narayana Murthy, the founder and former CEO of the company envisaged that the vision is in keeping the vision.

The company observed hesitation of young generations to come forth with their suggestions. On encouraging them to speak, Murthy found their suggestions and thoughts had a lot of substance and could help the company significantly. These people had not contributed to the discussions not because they had nothing of value to add, but because they were afraid of transgressing hierarchy. The hesitations bothered Murthy significantly and from this concern were born his grand plan to build a leadership institute that would groom and develop leaders from promising employees of Infosys (Infoscions), irrespective of hierarchy and give them the opportunity to shape the future of the company they were helping to build.

2. Leadership Development in Infosys: The company does not have any specific mechanism to identify leaders though it has a structured system of inculcating leadership capabilities within the recruits as well as experienced employees of all levels. The ILI ensures that talent is optimally harnessed to stay ahead of the innovation curve. Its dedicated campus in Mysore, India, offers courses on leadership and management. ILI groom high potential candidates under a three-tier mentoring process. Tier 1 includes business leaders and leaders of business enabler functions, Tier 2 has people who can take on Tier 1 responsibility in three to five years, and Tier 3 consists of Infoscions expected to reach Tier 1 category in six to ten years. Every Infocian in the leadership programme has a mentor. A member of the Board of Directors mentors a Tier 1 leader, whereas Tier 1 and Tier 2 leaders mentor Tier 2 and Tier 3 leaders respectively. As on 2006, Infosys have 51 leaders in Tier 1, 184 in Tier 2, and 427 in Tier 3. Other ILI initiatives are 'Pravesh', a program for first-time project managers, and the 'Global Business Finishing School'.

3. Nine Leadership Pillars: Infosys uses nine pillars for leadership development which are: (a) 360 degree feedback, (b) development assignments, (c) Infosys culture workshops, (d) development relationships, (e) leadership skills training, (f) feedback intensive programmes, (g) systemic process learning, (h) action learning, and (i) community empathy.

360 Degree Feedback: Multi-source assessment and feedback system emphasize the softer dimensions of performance like leadership, creativity, originality, innovation, teamwork, initiative, emotional intelligence, entrepreneurship, etc. This is the mechanism through which the company gathers data about an individual's performance and abilities. This information is collected from co-workers, including peers, subordinates, managers and customers. Personal development plans are prepared on the basis of this feedback. Then, each of these individuals is assigned an ILI faculty member to help prepare the personal development plan and to follow it.

Development Assignments: Infosys identify high potential employees (Infoscions) at various functions of the company and train them through job rotations and cross-functional assignments. This helps employees to acquire new leadership skills outside their own areas of expertise and experience.

Infosys Culture Workshops: These tailor-made workshops help to fortify and strengthen the Infosys culture amongst the participants, help instil better communication skills through sustained interaction amongst themselves, and identify with the values and processes involved in leadership development.

Development Relationships: The Company believes in healthy relationships among various levels of personnel. This includes one-on-one interaction in actual on-the-job work climate and leads to better sharing of knowledge and camaraderie amongst individuals. Mentoring forms an integral part of this exercise that strengthens the camaraderie or friendship.

Leadership Skills Training: The 'Leaders Teach Series' are workshops that the company's Tier-1 members, including Narayana Murthy (Chairman and Chief Mentor) and Nandan Nilekani (CEO and MD), hold to acclimatize the next rung with leadership roles and to groom them through their own rich experience.

Feedback Intensive Programmes: These are similar to 360-degree feedback, but based on formal and informal feedback from employees that an individual interacts with.

Systemic Process Learning: Infocians gain an overall view of the company and its diverse and complex systems, business, operations and processes. It is a continuous process and helps improve the individual and also the systems.

Action Learning: Infosys believe and encourage working in team. Action learning is an exercise constituting solving real problems in real-time conditions, but as a team.

Community Empathy: A company functions in a society. Infosys stresses the need to give back to society through involvement in various developmental, educational and social causes. This programme helps nurture a social conscience amongst its leaders.

4. Leadership Traits: The company is looking for the six leadership traits in its employees.

High Penetration for Self and Organization: An employee, a leader, can penetrate deeper through self-assessment which is a process to assess what one is doing, why he/she is doing it, and what he/she must do to improve the organization's performance. There are five essential questions to the process—What is our mission? Who is our customer?

What does the customer value? What are our results? What is our plan?

Passion for Excellence: Without enthusiasm and excitement of people an organization cannot gain excellence, become a role model, display value-based leadership, exhibit exemplary corporate governance, and so forth.

Team Player: Each team player must have role clarity, should know his/ her role and how his/her job fits in with the others. No matter what office politics are occurring, each team member must do the assigned work. If each person on the team makes a point to treat each member of the team with respect no matter what personal matters or matters of office politics are between them, they can still operate as team players working to get the job done

Desire in Learn Ability: Infosys, believing on continuous learning, inculcates the spirit of learnability among Infocians (as employees of Infosys are called) and an organizational commitment to continuous personal and professional development keeps. These keep Infosys at the forefront in a fast-changing industry.

Courage to Taking Risk: One cannot avoid taking risk in the work place. A person with high risk-taking propensity ultimately wins the game even if the playfield is the work area. But one should take calculated risk. A good leader has the courage to take risk. Of course, organizational environment matters.

Focus to Results and Attention to Details: The result or outcome and the process are important. Process approach to an activity helps to complete that with perfection.

5. Nine Dimensions of Leadership: Infosys believes that the leadership must drive the creation of a leadership funnel at different levels of the organization, must be cantered on the infocians, and must be rooted in the organizational context. There cannot be any single mantra to develop the leadership that needs multiple methods and multiple directions. Strategic leadership, change leadership, operational leadership, talent leadership, relationship/networking leadership, content leadership, entrepreneurial leadership, transactional leadership, and adversity leadership are the nine dimensions Infosys is looking for. These nine dimensions are explained for in-depth understanding whatever the nature of business is.

Strategic Leadership: It is about unique positioning; how one can create a unique position of the company. Strategic leadership is about creating an agile and flexible organization, which can cope to changes in the business environment and suitably respond to that.

Change Leadership: It is about changing the context and making change effective. A leader, particularly a top level leader, must have the vision to anticipate the direction and speed of changes in the business environment. Accordingly, he/she has to finalize steps to set up changes in the organization, communicate the reasons behind the internal changes to various levels of personnel. While incorporating the changes many issues would emerge which he/she must handle combining firmness and flexibility.

Operational Leadership: It is about achieving high degree of effectiveness and productivity. This leadership refers to defining the operational excellence in the organizational context; considering the framework used to achieve the operational excellence and judging the used parameters for rightness.

Talent Leadership: It is about creating top quality leadership team; globally best in class in the relevant area. A top level manager must understand the need of nurturing talents and he has to develop system to identify talents of middle and junior level managers and provide them with required inputs so that their potentials are realized. A top level organizational leader has to see himself as a teacher or coach and devote time to develop next levels of leaders.

Relationship/Networking Leadership: It is about building bridges of relationship, developing, maintaining and leveraging long-term internal and external relationship networks. In fact, relationships operate at different levels in an organization and with various influential agencies who can impact the business. A leader must understand the difference between breadth and depth of relationship grid. A suitable communication strategy needs to go hand in hand in relation building strategy.

Content Leadership: It is about thought leadership; whatever can be applied for intellectual property rights. Content leadership needs assessing the level of domain expertise of the business. The domain can be banking, insurance, advertising, software development, etc. If the domain is banking technology the content includes core banking, internet banking, and customer relation management.

Entrepreneurial Leadership: It is about having entrepreneurial zeal and showing ownership for business outcomes. The entrepreneurial zeal of a manager takes him from humdrum and monotonous state to elsewhere when he can contribute effectively to the organization. This skill encompasses power of imagination and commitment in the face of challenges.

Transactional Leadership: It is about acquiring and integrating new lines of business. Transactional leaders create clear structures whereby it is clear what is required of their subordinates, and the rewards that they get for following orders. They do not always mention punishment for non-conformance or if the things go wrong. The transactional leader often uses management by exception, working on the principle that if something is operating to expected and defined performance level then it does not need attention. Beyond expectation, performances require praise and reward for exceeding expectation, whilst some kind of corrective action is applied for performance below expectation.

Adversity Leadership: Adversity may arise from multiple types of differences in region, religion, language spoken, gender, belief system, cultural and social backgrounds, etc. adversity is part and parcel of any business organization. It can be small or big and is likely to impede the functioning of business. As a leader, you have to handle the adversity whatever be the intensity. A leader learns from his experiences and initiates steps to prevent recurrence of such situations. However, Infosys has adversity centre to manage problems arising out of diversity.

6. Leadership Journey: Infosys selects high potential personnel through structured systems. The leadership journey starts from this point as the company keeps track of their performances. It identifies a pool of employees (Infocians) on the basis of past performances and leadership potential. The duration of leadership is long enough. Company classifies a segment of Infocians as 'high potentials'. One ILI faculty member is attached with each high potential employee who guides to leadership journey and helps to develop. The faculty member provides all round support in implementing the individual change objectives. All high potential employees are trained at ILI. The faculty member acts as coach, mentor, counsellor, and internal consultants to enhance the enabling capacities capable to undertake complex assignments and resolve real business issues efficiently and effectively.

Concluding Remarks

Business environment is dwindling. Leadership styles duly considers emotional intelligence base. To survive and grow any company needs capable leaders who can transform. Leaders need a set of skills comprising time management, delegation, managing conflict, persuasiveness, negotiation, problem solving, technical competency, goal setting. Leadership development is the need of the day. Leaders must be assertive.

Organisations are required to have talent management system and employ the talent management continuum. Activities to manage talents must be defined and documented. Leaders should know their followers. Fostering creativity is imperative to gain competitive advantages. Organisational leaders must encourage working in teams to make best use of collective intelligence, collective wisdom, and collective consciousness. Empowerment and accountability manifest their importance to instil responsibility within managers. Training and development interventions must be meticulously planned to take delivery of return on investment. Structured leadership development programmes are essential to promote skills and competencies. Students are managers and engineers of the future. Young managers are likely to ascend to the top management level. We need to make the doll when the clay is soft.

References

Belbin, R. M. (1981), *Management Team Why they Succeed or Fail*, Heineman, London.

Haldar, U.K. and Juthika, S. (2012), *Human Resource Management*, Oxford Higher Education, Oxford University Press, New Delhi.

Haldar, U.K. (2009), *Human Resource Development*, Oxford Higher Education, Oxford University Press India, New Delhi.

Haldar, U.K. (2010), *Leadership and Team Building*, Oxford Higher Education, Oxford University Press India, New Delhi.

Howell, J.P. and Costley, D.L. (2006), *Understanding Behaviours for Effective Leadership*, Prentice-Hall of India Private Limited, New Delhi.

Hughes, R.L., Ginnett, R.C. and Curphy, G.J. (2008), *Leadership Enhancing the Lessons of Experience*, Tata McGraw-Hill Publishing Company Limited, New Delhi.

Kindersley, D. (2000), *Negotiating Skills*, Dorling Kindersley Limited, New York.

Macdonald, C. (2008), *A Brief Introduction to Collective Wisdom*, www.wisdompage.com, accessed on November 16, 2008.

Majumdar, S. and Lesliy, D. (2008), Down to Earth, *Indian Management*, November, 47(11), 22-30.

Schimmel, D. (1976), www.psychologicalselfhelp.org.

Telsang, Martand (2002), *Human Dimension of Total Quality Management*, Indian Society for Training and Development, New Delhi.

4

Personnel Selection: Issues and Challenges

Vijay Parkash and Updesh Kumar

Introduction

Personnel selection, as the term itself indicates, is a process with the main objective of identification of potential, efficient and competent candidates who fit to the requirements of the target job and can substantially and significantly contribute to the particular organization in enhancing its productivity and flourishing overall growth. In short, the primary objective of effective personnel selection is to make the decision about who the right person is (for any particular job), by matching individual characteristics (ability, experience, and training) with the specific job and organizational requirements.

If this objective of 'personnel selection' is not met adequately and if appropriate person-job fit is not achieved by selectors, it may be an obstruction in the growth of both employee as well as the organization as both will not be able to satisfy each-other's expectations or needs of job satisfaction and effective employee performance. (Robbins and Judge, 2011) Hence, it is believed by most of the experts that the most important human resource decision an organizational leader or manager makes is about deciding who to recruit for the job. (Noe, 2012) Therefore, this issue of personnel selection has been a prominent area of concern among the organizational psychologists, human resource professionals and managers who have 'personnel selection' as their primary function.

In their pursuit to optimally contribute towards organization's growth, the selectors put their best possible efforts and try to utilize the best possible selection methodologies for choosing the right personnel. In this process, based on our long personal experience of involvement in personnel selection in the form of assessing several thousand candidates appearing for the positions of officers in Indian Armed Forces and being as policy makers for the same, we can say that most of the professionals encounter a question: which is the best method for selecting right personnel and why? Although the recruiters or selectors have to ultimately adapt to any one kind of method or approach for selecting the personnel, they have to first go through analyzing various existing methodologies to evaluate the effectiveness and preference of one over the other.

The issues related to validity, reliability, time consumption, cost, ease in administration etc have to be kept in the loop of analysis along with the knowledge of limitations and strengths of different kind of assessment methodologies. The present article is an attempt to address various issues and the possible challenges in front of the professionals involved in personnel selection in various organizations. Though there is no dearth of literature on the issues related to personnel selection, the following text in this chapter is an effort to briefly delineate upon various issues and challenges in personnel selection in general and the utility and critical evaluation of various selection approaches in particular. We believe that few pages of a chapter cannot suffice to address all issues in personnel selection and to provide the solution to all the challenges in this field; therefore, our approach in this chapter will be more towards igniting the readers' mind with more of queries rather than providing answers.

Testing versus Assessment

Often, the matter of concern for psychologists is objective description of behaviour or personnel attributes. The processes or operations utilized to objectively assess and describe people's behaviour or attributes are generally referred as measurement. (Berdie, Layton, Swanson and Hagenah, 1963; p. 69) The early workers in the area of psychological measurement, Berdie et al. (1963), believe that in their efforts to objectively describe the behaviour, the behavioural scientists generally face a problem of constructing an efficient framework in which the behaviour of an individual or a sample of his behaviour (attributes) can be described objectively.

The procedure that we utilize to solve the mentioned problem is broadly referred to as *testing*, wherein psychologists are often concerned with prediction of future behaviour by means of measuring the present characteristics of the individual that are inferred from the individual's responses to a given situation at a given moment. In psychological testing it is assumed that every kind of response represents some kind of behavioural correlates. (Berdie et al., 1963)

The terms psychological testing and *assessment* are used interchangeably for majority of the times. Although psychological *assessment* is similar to psychological *testing*, it usually involves a more comprehensive assessment of the individual.

While testing, in its objective sense, is restricted to use of tests to measure any sample of behaviour, assessment is a broader term that involves the integration of information from multiple sources such as different kinds of tests as well as information from personal interviews, bio data analysis, observations, family histories and so forth.

After being aware of the difference between simple testing and detailed assessment, should the candidates' assessment in personnel selection be restricted to objective *testing?* If it is restricted to objective tests, which type of tests should be employed on the candidates? Will only psychological tests be sufficient to provide all necessary information? Why detailed *assessment* by gathering information should or should not be used? If it should be used, which all sources of information should be relied upon to get the requisite information about the candidate? How do other factors like reliability and validity of information sources, cost, time, information availability and training of the selectors to objectively evaluate the available information by means of different sources, and so forth, influence the decisions regarding opting for simple testing of the candidates or in-depth assessment? And, how to find the best possible answers of these raised questions? Furthermore, there can be numerous similar questions and challenges in front of the professionals in the field of personnel selection; and again another question is raised—what are those? Now let us try to provide the readers with certain possible directions to find the answers of the raised queries.

As far as the use of objective tests is concerned, it is well evident to almost everyone that there is a requirement of different construct specific tests for assessing different aspects of behaviour. We are sure that most of the professionals in the field, believe that no single psychological test can provide complete information regarding a candidate's all personnel attributes that are required to be successful on the job. Then, should the selectors use number of objective tests to get the complete picture of one's attributes? If yes, then which all attributes should be the target of assessment—personality traits, intelligence, cognitive abilities, interest, leadership and managerial qualities, interpersonal skills, emotional intelligence or something else?

Providing support to the idea of utilizing objective tests, Lunenburg (2011) opines that testing is believed to be the single best selection device across jobs by many human resource experts. Putting forth the advantages of testing, Hunt (2008) asserts that testing is advantageous in finding the right person for the job, attainment of high degree of job satisfaction for the applicant due to the person-organization goodness of fit, and reducing absenteeism and enhancing productivity and turnover. In order to get better person-job fit, the use of intelligence tests, personality tests, and interest inventories can prove very helpful to the leaders in their most crucial decision of personnel selection. (Lunenburg, 2011)

However the emphasis of Lunenburg (2011) is more on psychological tests, he also believes that in the selection process of most organizations "the most common procedure involves a series of steps including biographical information, reference checks, interviews, written tests, and performance simulations" (p. 1) that supports the notion of using detailed *assessment* rather than limiting to psychological tests. Most of the organizations adopt a multifaceted approach by basing their personnel selection on getting maximum information about the candidates by detailed assessment mostly by means of a combination of bio-data analysis, psychological tests and personal interviews. Let us now attempt to address the issues and challenges concerning to these three.

Bio-data Analysis

In the domain of personnel selection and performance research, the use of information about life experiences is supported by the evidence that an individual's future behaviour is strongly influenced by his past (Owens, 1976; Owens and Schoenfeldt, 1979), to the extent that past behaviours and experiences can provide significant guiding path to predict future behaviours and experiences. This above postulation is embedded in the *consistency principle*, which argues that the best forecaster of prospect behaviour is precedent behaviour. (Owens, 1976; Wernimont and Campbell, 1968) Assuming so does not mean that future events repeat or imitate past events, however it implies that they are conditioned by the past and affect the likelihood of a specific behaviour in a new and emergent situation. (Mumford and Stokes, 1992)

Bio data is generally described as the information about the personal life-history and experience of an individual that is provided in the form of applications for employment and resumes. The information available in bio-data is presumed to be related to occupational success and is considered to be a predictor of certain work-related behaviours. (Gunter, Furnham and Drakeley, 1993) Experts in the area believe that the events occurring in one's life are quite useful in assessing the type of people willing to join any particular occupation as the bio-data can predict vocational choice of an individual through his personality development patterns. (Nickels, 1990; Schneider and Schneider, 1990)

It is also believed that bio-data information is an indicator of consistency for any employment role over a period of time and employee's demographic information and other material in a job application can predict turnover and tenure in most organizations. (Schneider and Schneider, 1990; Rothstein, Erwin, Schmidt and Owens, 1990) Gunter and colleagues (1993) assert that when used correctly bio-data are among the best recruitment devices. Nickels (1994), another prominent researcher in the field of bio-data, opined that measures of bio-data can predict performance across many aspects of behaviour and they in fact do so since responses to bio-data items may serve to incarcerate previous manifestations of the constructs and mechanisms that eventually determine prognostic relationships with criteria.

If we go by the assumptions and assertions cited above, we can certainly accept that bio-data are crucial tools of personnel selection; however, in order to make them more effective, Nickels (1994) stated that it is essential to obtain an understanding of the type of constructs that contribute to the prognostic power of bio-data measures. Also, the construction of any background or demographic data measure must focus on the developmental antecedents of effective job performance. (Mumford and Owens, 1987) Lot of emphasis is given to bio-data measures and it is evident that almost all kind of organizations and jobs in the very first step seek the bio-data of the candidates.

Still, the question arises that in order to consider or make bio-data the best recruitment devices what all information should be sought in the bio-data measures? Are bio-data measures actually *standardized* tools? How do selectors draw inferences about future performance based on information in bio-data? Do the selectors adopt a *standard* and *objective* methodology in analyzing the bio-data information? Are bio-data based predictions actually reliable and valid? Furthermore, there can be many other questions relating to the requirements to specialized training to the interpreters, the relative cost and time factors and so forth. All these queries though seem very simple and directly answerable but these queries are the serious issues of debate among the professionals posing amicable challenge to the personnel selection as a whole. Although we are putting lot of questions in front of the readers' minds, we are not denying the importance of these tools. However, simultaneous to assigning importance to the bio-data measures, the importance of the other approaches comprising psychological tests and interviews can also not be underestimated.

Use of Psychological Tests

There is a long history of use of written tests as selection devices and majority of organizations do utilize testing to hire people. It has been revealed on the basis of a comprehensive survey conducted on 2,500 organizations in the United States that use of tests is considered as a primary device to make hiring and promotion related decisions in more than 60 percent of the organizations. (Guion, 2010) Most of the human resource experts believe that in comparison to bio-data information and interviews psychological tests provide more information about a job applicant, and they are less subject to subjective biases.

Still, few issues should necessarily bother the mind of the professions regarding which all abilities are required to be assessed and which type of tests should be used.

Edenborough (2008) classified the many kinds of tests available for organization use into three major groups that are: (a) intelligence or cognitive ability tests, (b) personality tests, and (c) interest inventories. Besides the three categories of tests, specific subject matter knowledge testing other than the basic intellectual capability also makes a part of personnel selection procedures in many organizations. Knowledge testing may have specified curriculum but what about the target constructs tapped in the three categories of tests mentioned previously?

Further, how do we decide about those target constructs? The probable answer to these questions lies in the concept of job analysis. Job analysis for any specific position in an organization may provide the descriptions of the exact nature of duties to be carried out by the employees, the specific knowledge component required for successful completion of any task as a part of the given duty, and may the specific personality traits and interests that are again confined to performing a specified job in particular. But, does the job analysis cover all aspects of the organization and employee satisfaction? How do the professionals assess the needs and expectations of the employees from organizations? These are minor issues that may be dealt with by simply paying more attention to the scope of functioning of an employee in the organization as a whole rather than on a specified duty he will be performing. In case these issues remain unresolved, there is no doubt that these will emerge as bigger challenges in future taking the shape of dissatisfaction on the part of employee and in turn lesser productivity of the organization.

Intelligence Tests

Different types of jobs have different demands required of employees in respect to use of their intellectual abilities (Lunenburg, 2011). Tests of intellectual abilities or *Intelligence tests* have proven to be very good prognostic yardsticks for jobs requiring the employees to perform mental activities, such as thinking, reasoning, and problem solving. (Gregory, 2007) In general, intelligence tests measure an individual's general intellectual abilities in terms of intelligence quotient (IQ). More or higher level of general intelligence will be required to perform well on a job that is more complex in terms of thinking, reasoning, and problem-solving skills. (Groth-Marnat, 2010) High intelligence is not as important and prerequisite for highly routine jobs that have few information-processing demands.

It appears as if there are no issues as far as the assessment of intellectual capabilities is concerned; few questions that may be important in one way or other need to be looked into by the professionals. Is mere IQ index sufficient to predict the level of all cognitive abilities? Or, do we need to assess more cognitive abilities? If yes, which other abilities should be assessed by the personnel selectors in addition to general intelligence? Numerous psychological tests are available to measure the same attribute of a person. Which tests should the selectors use and why? And, should it be a performance test or paper-pencil test? Furthermore, a current line of research in psychology believes that standard intelligence plays minor role in successful performance on the job and it is the *emotional intelligence* that plays major role. (Goleman, 1995)

Though we wiii deliberate on the issues of emotional intelligence in the proceeding sections, considering the second line of thought as an important one seeing plethora of research on emotional intelligence, another question arises—how much impetus should be given to general intelligence testing? Or should we do away with it and concentrate on emotional intelligence testing? Such types of issues might have even been raised by some other professionals and raising these issues cannot be a reason to ignore the importance of intellectual abilities. However, these concerns will help researchers help the organizations by finding out the valid answers of these questions by means of future researches.

Personality Tests

Although the crucial importance of cognitive ability tests cannot be denied, relatively fewer companies use them as selection tools despite the evident predictive validity and high efficacy provided by cognitive ability testing. The primary reason behind this avoidance of use of cognitive ability measures in personnel selection by some organizations is the research evidence that demonstrates that cognitive ability testing reveals group or racial differences or adverse impact. (Cleary, Humphreys, Kendrick and Wesman, 1975; Hartigan and Wigdor, 1989; Wigdor and Gamer, 1982) Researchers have advocated adding a personality test to an ability test as a means of enhancing validity while reducing adverse impact of the selection system. The assumption underlying this argument is that there are factors related to job performance other than cognitive ability and that using these factors to predict job success produces less adverse impact. If these alternative factors are included with cognitive ability in a selection battery, then adverse impact should be significantly reduced. (Thomas and Scroggins, 2006). But, are personality measures valid predictors of job performance?

"While the utility of cognitive ability testing in personnel selection has been broadly accepted, the utility of personality testing, until relatively recently, has not". (Thomas and Scroggins, 2006, p. 33) Hogan, Hogan, and Roberts (1996) documented that the application of personality tests as the tools for personnel selection has been challenged by many researches that reveal their low predictive validity and the susceptibility to invasion of privacy based on item content. (cited by Thomas and Scroggins, 2006) Additionally, "the lack of agreement regarding the components of personality, the many different types of personality instruments available, and the inappropriate application of clinical instruments to selection have contributed to the reluctance of many organizations to apply personality testing to employee selection". (Thomas and Scroggins, 2006, p. 33)

An important review of the available research by Guion and Gottier (1965) has most often become the basis of the momentum for many meta-analytic studies of personality-job performance relations. Guion and Gottier (1965), on the basis of their review, concluded that there was little evidence for the validity of personality measures in the field of personnel selection. This review raised a big debate in the arena of personality and personnel selection research and hundreds of later research articles challenged the conclusion given by Guion and Gottier and attempted to demonstrate the validity of numerous personality constructs in predicting job performance in many diverse occupations and by means of a variety of performance criteria.

Two meta-analytic studies of personality-job performance relations have been especially influential. Barrick and Mount (1991) in their study estimated true correlation between five-factor model dimensions of personality and performance across both occupational groups. Although the correlations were relatively modest, these results provided an optimistic view of the prospective role of personality traits in forecasting job performance and this study had significant influence on researchers and practitioners. (Mount and Barrick, 1998; Murphy, 2000) Tett, Jackson and Rothstein (1991) carried out a meta-analysis of personality-job performance relations to show the critical importance of a confirmatory research strategy to validity research, in which personality measures were hypothesized to be linked to specific job performance criteria.

These studies provided a clearer insight in the role of personality attributes in job performance by examining the effects of personality traits on different criterion job types and in different occupations. Thus, results from Barrick and Mount (1991) and Tett and colleagues (1991) became the base for a regeneration of interest in both research and practice with respect to the use of personality to predict work related behaviour. Extending the research further, Raja, Johns and Ntalianis (2004) assert that personality traits may have noteworthy impact on the types of psychological contracts between employee and employer.

Personality tests are used in the organizations from long back as measure one's healthy personality attributes. In recent past, the use of personality tests has increased many folds and today almost every organization attempts to understand the incumbents' personality before recruiting them. Through *personality tests* an attempt is made to measure various personality attributes that may be important on the job, such as conscientiousness, emotional stability, introversion and extroversion, aggressiveness or submissiveness, self-confidence, leadership qualities, and many other traits and attributes. (Cattell, 2010) Many theoretical models explaining personality in terms of different types and traits are used by different organizations.

In particular, many organizations use the five broad dimensions and their underlying 30 facets of the Five-Factor Model of personality for making selection related decisions. (Judge, Bono, Ilies and Gerhardt, 2002) Going by this majority connotation of use of the five-factor model, conscientiousness and emotional stability are the traits that best predict the job performance. (Barrick and Mount, 2004) Though the facet composition of these two dimensions covers few of the essential traits that help a person perform better at any front, there remains a matter of debate about the preferential use of one personality descriptive model over the other whereas most of the personality models correlate significantly to each other in one way or other.

When numerous personality theories and models are existing–some describing personality in form of 16 type, some in the form of 16 personality factors or six factors or five factors, some in three factors and likewise many others–it also makes an issue of concern–should we go by a predetermined personality model and try to fit it in the job requirements? Or, should we go for in-depth job analysis and determine the requisite personality traits on the basis of job-analysis? The issue is open to the human resource professionals with the evident facts of efforts, time and money requirements of job-analysis coupled with direct robust linkage to the particular job and organizational requirements vis-à-vis saving of efforts, time and money due to in hand models coupled with only inferential linkage with job and organizational requirements. Once the issue of target traits is resolved, the question arises– which type of tests should the professionals use—objective tests or projective tests or in combination? There are certain inherent issues with each kind of tests.

Projective tests are particularly sensitive to unconscious characteristics of behaviour. Projective tests are highly multidimensional in nature, encourage a wide variety of responses and thereby reveal maximum latitude of one's personality make-up. These tests allow free responding on the part of the individual and the individual is not aware of the purpose of the tests. In comparison to the projective tests, *objective tests* consist of restricted type of response pattern and have an objective method of scoring and interpretation. These objective tests generally include statements, or questions wherein the subject responds in a particular pattern desired by the test. Now the questions arise that which of the two, that is projective and objective tests, should be used in personnel selection. There are two sides of both these coins.

On the one hand projective tests provide more significant information but are more time and effort consuming and on the other hand objective tests are time and effort saving but their scope remains restricted in terms of measurement of any single particular construct for which they are meant. Therefore, though majority of the organizations use objective tests in personnel selection, it is still a dilemma as which one will the best and what are the basis of professionals' preference to one over the other? When this issue is deliberated upon, consequently the issue of reliability and validity of these measures also becomes a matter of concern.

It is a well evident fact that projective tests provide a richer data as far as personality assessment is concerned; still projective tests are generally used for clinical and diagnostic purposes and very rarely in personnel selection. Even for the clinical and diagnoses purposes, and even after due credit to the projective approach, some projective tests are less often used today because they are more time consuming to administer and their reliability and validity are criticized a lot. Firstly, they are prone to subjective biases of the raters and secondly due to absence of any readily available criteria about the real time information inferred their validity is considered more a hypothetical one rather than being really predictive.

However, many practitioners continue to rely on projective testing as due to the richness of available unconscious information they may also be useful in drawing inferences to follow-up with other methods. In comparison to projective tests, objective measures are hardly criticized for their psychometric properties and they are free from subjective biases at all stages of testing. So, what is the best approach for choosing the best test type?

During the last decade, interest of professionals has recently surged in the class of tests known as *situational judgment tests* (SJTs). Situational judgment tests comprise of many job-relevant situations where in the job applicant has to make a judgment about different aspects of the situation and he has to respond to the demands of the presented practical situation. The effectiveness of the judgment and response serves as an indicator of prospective job performance. Although use of situational judgment tests is not a new idea, in recent decades they were independently reintroduced under differing labels and found a receptive audience.

While some scholars present the situations in the form of 'low fidelity simulations' (Motowidlo, Dunnette and Carter, 1990), some (e.g. Wagner and Sternberg, 1985) framed SJTs as measures of 'tacit knowledge' and 'practical intelligence'. Similarly, for different purposes either behavioural-tendency instructions are preferred or knowledge-based instructions are preferred. Whatever be the format, currently many professionals consider SJTs as a potential supplement to ability and personality measures (Sackett and Lievens, 2008) and recommend their use in personnel selection. Now the human resource professionals are again left with the task of comparison of SJTs with other types of tests and decide about the preferred type of tests to be used for personnel selection. Should they use SJTs rather than objective tests? If yes, should the SJTs be having low fidelity simulations or should they tap tacit and practical knowledge? Should the response pattern be behavioural-tendency based or should it be knowledge-based? Likewise, there can be countless such questions that pose a challenge of getting best possible answers, but more important than anything else is the issue of reliability and validity of different types of tests.

Reliability and Validity of Measures

"The field of psychological testing has not been exempt from the influence of fads and the introduction of ineffective tools, particularly in the manner tests are used and test results interpreted". (Thomas and Scroggins, 2006, p. 30) As far as the psychological testing in employment arena is concerned, professional psychologists have continuously cautioned about new trends and weaker tools. (Dawes, 1994; Dunette, 1966; Dunette and Hough, 1992; Lubinski, 1996)

Being concerned about the usage of scientifically based methodologies to human resource selection seems to be quite logical as the field of personnel selection has struggled with both methods and outcomes in attempts to identify and avail the measurement tools which can fulfil the need for scientific rigor and which can be readily accepted by practitioners on the basis of their utility. (Thomas and Scroggins, 2006) This struggle of the human resource professionals comes coupled with their concerns about the psychometric properties of those instruments or testing methods. Only a reliable and valid tool can be considered scientifically rigorous. The issue that emerges now is about the extent and particular method of reliability or validity.

Reliability which is often understood in terms of consistency of scores is also known to represent the true and error free score of an individual on any particular attribute. Therefore, a relevant issue in front of human resource personnel and even test developers can be that which meaning should actually be adhered to. Furthermore, though fundamentally focusing on the similar or rather same property, there are different types of reliability estimates. Then, which is the best indicator of reliability in true sense of provision of error free scores? What if the score or results are consistent but include a constant component of error? Specific to use of projective tests, is it possible to actually tap the exact component of error in assessment of any particular attribute if there is perfect inter-rater agreement but with a constant systematic error?

It is understandable that in statistical terms we can simply ignore the constant error or can consider it null and void, what if this error is contributing to the latency or lack in measurement of any particular job specific attribute? Making reliability an essential condition for validity, this question connects both psychometric properties of reliability and validity to each other, and the constant error component seems to be pertaining more to the validity aspect.

Similar to reliability, the *validity* of measures used for selecting personnel is of crucial importance to successful personnel selection practice. (Cascio and Aguinis, 2005) However, validity in general means to fulfilment of purpose, the exact sense of understanding validity varies depending on the types of measurement tools used, the situation, and the exact operationalization of the target constructs. Simultaneously, as most of us are aware that there are different types of validity including content validity, criterion validity and construct validity with each having further subtypes, which should be the one on which the professional should rely while using any measure to recruit people?

Criterion validity is generally considered better for performance prediction but should it be based on the data from job applicants (predictive validity) or on the data from current successful employees (concurrent validity)? While making all these crucial decisions, selectors need to keep in mind that any specific measurement instrument can have different validities according to different yardsticks or ways in which performance can be defined (Cascio and Aguinis, 2005), including the time taken by an employee to learn a job, the job tenure, work output, or employee attitudes.

Further, it is also a matter of concern for the professionals that prior to the criterion administration, they need to decide about the other validity indices including content and construct aspects along with convergent and discriminant properties. The issue of generalization of validities across different jobs and situations within same organization also bothers the minds of selectors and puts forth a significant challenge to make inferential decisions with the same resource instruments. These basic decisions pose significant challenges in front of the selectors specifically due to the mandatory presence of uncontrollable or very partially controllable aspects of socially desirable responding or faking good.

Psychologists are generally aware of the fact that most of the psychological tests, with a minor exception to projective measures, are not free from certain kinds of *response biases* and distortions. Researchers believe that response bias or response distortion is the most frequent criticism of personality measures used in personnel selection. (Ones, Viswesvaran and Reiss, 1996) *Response distortion* has largely been described as social desirability, impression management, faking, intentional distortion, self deception and self enhancement. (Hough et al., 1990; Ones et al., 1996) Response distortion is the systematic tendency to respond in such a way that interferes with accurate assessment. Response distortions may be in the form of *response styles* denoting biases that are consistent across time and questionnaires, or *response sets* indicating short-lived response biases attributable to some temporary distraction or motivation. (Lanyon and Goodstein, 1997 and Paulhus, 1991)

Other than response styles or response sets, *socially*

desirable responding is considered as a tendency to deliberately or unconsciously respond in such a way that is considered approvable in any particular context present oneself in a favourable light. Early researchers believe that socially desirable responding is the tendency to give overly positive self descriptions and refers to a manner of presenting oneself in a favourable light. (Crowne and Marlowe, 1960) When this tendency is deliberate rather than being unconscious this deliberate misrepresentation is termed as 'faking good'. (Furnham and Henderson, 1982)

We believe that professionals in personnel selection are well aware of the fact that it is not possible to completely control the influence of socially desirable responding or faking good. In that case, it is a matter of concern for selectors that they need to be aware of the factors causing faking good and socially desirable responding. It also becomes evident that in case of cultures like India that give more impetus on social conformity and group behaviours social desirability is a learned aspect and a part of one habit strengths. Further, instruments with higher face validities will invite more faking. Therefore, controlling or measuring the influence of socially desirable responding and faking is another challenge in front of the selectors. How do we control or measure social desirability and faking? Are the tests of socially desirable responding or the lie scales sufficient? Or, is the use of projective tests the possible solution? These queries reverse the thought process of the human resource personnel and there is a need to again look back to basics in order to meet these challenges and resolve the issues.

Alternative Assessment Measures

Though major part of assessment in personnel selection includes testing of cognitive abilities and personality attributes by means of employing psychological tests, in many of the organizations the information received by means of tests is supplemented by interest inventories, interviews, and more recently performance simulations. *Interest inventories*, as the name indicates, attempt to tap an applicant's interest in performing various kinds of activities that he will probably be facing on the job. The administration of interest tests to job applicants works on the assumption that certain people perform jobs well because the job activities are interesting. (Hogan, 2007) But after assessing the cognitive abilities requisite to the job, the aptitude and requisite personality traits, do we actually need to assess the interest of the applicants or are we simply increasing the load of human resource personnel? Is their application for the job itself not an indicative of their interest?

These are minor issues the resolution of which will probably lessen the burden of the selectors. In the recent times, assessing a sample of performance in simulated conditions is also used in some organizations to improve the selection of competent personnel by having them perform part of the job. This small performance simulation helps determine whether the candidates have the potential to do the job successfully. *Performance simulations* are generally considered as predictors of whether applicants can do the job successfully. (Thomas and Scroggins, 2006) There is no doubt that performance simulations demonstrate applicant's skills in that particular moment of time, but the challenge that still remains in front of the selectors is about the extent of prediction regarding surety of future performance.

Interview is most commonly used device in personnel selection along with the psychological tests. Interviews may be structured, semi-structured (in the form of interview schedules) or unstructured. Now the issues that emerge are—which out of the three is the best approach of interview? Hough and Oswald (2000) believe that structured employment interviews are better than the unstructured ones because they define content more explicitly. "Their successes are therefore more likely to replicate, and they are better analyzed and meta-analyzed to determine their transportability to other jobs and work settings". (Hough and Oswald, 2000, p. 641) Does that mean that structured interviews should be used more? However, researchers (e.g., Graves and Karren 1996) believe that organizations still prefer unstructured interviews over the structured ones.

On the other hand, structured interviews are considered to have higher inter-rater reliability than unstructured interviews. (Conway, Jako and Goodman, 1995) They are considered legally defensible; there is lesser requirement of particularly trained skills; they are less susceptible to rating biases (Kataoka, Latham and Whyte, 1997); they have better validity (Schmidt and Rader 1999); and, they are fairer in the sense of treating applicants in consistent manner. (Hough and Oswald, 2000) Even after these many advantages—why do professionals prefer unstructured interviews? Are they correct in doing this? If the interview will be so much structured then what will be the difference between interview and tests? Will an unstructured interview not elicit more information? Should the professionals be more bothered about structure or about gathering more information or about both? These are few of the issues that we put before the personnel selectors. To evaluate the probable answers of these questions we wish to supplement the reader with the assertions of the researchers that interviewee characteristics like hand movement and physical appearance, even when coded independent of the content, are considered predictors of several dimensions of managerial effectiveness. (Burnett and Motowidlo, 1998)

Extending the discussion about alternative assessment supplements, it seems plausible to discuss with the professionals about a recent line of research that has taken shape in the last two decades and places impetus on another attribute named emotional intelligence that is, though distinct but, more close to the domain of personality traits. Pertaining to the awareness, understanding and management of one's own and others' emotions (Goleman, 1995; Mayer and Salovey, 1997; Bar*On*, 1997), emotional intelligence is considered to be playing majority and significant role in success in all aspects of life. Two of the pioneers in this field Goleman (1995, 1998) and Bar*O*n, (1997) believe that emotional intelligence enables a person to understand and manage one's and other's emotions and handling interpersonal relationships which is an essential contributor in coping with daily life situations.

Ample amount of researches exist and most of the scholars and researchers have empirically validated the significance of the role of emotional intelligence in organizational effectiveness and successful job performance. Hence, the consideration of assessment of this important construct by professionals in personnel selection is again an issue to be looked into when already many organizations are assessing it at time of recruitment. Further, if importance is assigned to its assessment—which model should be adopted and why? Should the professional focus on it in terms of ability or should they focus on it considering it something within the personality domain? Human resource managers in the organizations are considered to have better emotional intelligence and therefore it is better to leave these issues in the domain of their thinking and in purview of their problem solving abilities to meet these challenges.

Final Note

Personnel selection is such a broad area of study, research and application that it is truly a big challenge for the professionals to make optimum use of knowledge existing in this domain. As we began with the note of keeping the focus of this chapter limited to raising issues and challenges for the human resource professionals working in the field of personnel selection, we also mentioned that our motive is to ignite the minds of the professionals by raising more of questions rather than providing answers. Though appreciating the vastness of the subject matter of personnel selection it is not an easy task to address all the issues and concerns, we have tried left certain unanswered questions in the domain of human resource professionals and researchers. We have attempted to document the most prevalent personnel selection methodologies along with certain guiding inputs regarding making crucial decisions while hiring employees. It is now up to the readers to provide knowledgeable inputs about whether the concerns raised by us are crucial to personnel selection or not; and, how we can optimize personnel selection approaches by addressing the raised issues and challenges.

References

BarOn, R. (1997), *The Emotional Quotient Inventory (EQ-i): Technical Manual.* Toronto: Multi Health Systems.

Barrick, M.R. and Mount, M.K. (1991), The Big Five Personality Dimensions and Job Performance: A Meta-analysis. *Personnel Psychology, 44*(1), 1-26.

Barrick, M.R. and Mount, M.K. (2004), Select on Conscientiousness and Emotional Stability, in E.A. Locke (ed.), *Handbook of Principles of Organizational Behaviour,* pp. 15-28, Malden, MA: Blackwell.

Berdie, R.F., Layton, W.L., Swanson, E.O. and Hagenah, T. (1963), *Testing in Guidance and Counselling.* New York: McGraw-Hill.

Burnett, J.R., and Motowidlo, S.J. (1998), Relations between Different Sources of Information in the Structured Selection Interview, *Personnel Psychology, 51,* 963-983.

Cascio, W.F., and Aguinis, H. (2005), *Applied Psychology in Human Resource Management* (6th ed.), Upper Saddle River, NJ: Pearson Prentice Hall.

Cattell, R. (2010), *The Scientific Analysis of Personality,* Piscataway, NJ: Transaction.

Cleary, T.A, Humphreys, L.G., Kendrick, S.A. and Wesman, A. (1975), Educational Uses of Tests with Disadvantaged Students, *American Psychologist, 30,* 15-41.

Conway, J.M., Jako, R.A. and Goodman, D.F. (1995), A Meta-analysis of Inter-rater and Internal Consistency Reliability of Selection Interviews, *Journal of Applied Psychology, 80,* 565-579.

Crowne, D.P. and Marlowe, D. (1960), A New Scale of Social Desirability Independent of Psychopathology, *Journal of Consulting Psychology, 24,* 349-354.

Dawes, R. M. (1994), *House of Cards*. New York: Macmillan.

DeRue, D.S. and Morgeson, F.P. (2007), Stability and Change in Person-team and Person-role Fit Overtime: The Effects of Growth Satisfaction, Performance, and General self-efficacy. *Journal of Applied Psychology, 92*(5), 1242-1253.

Dunnette, M.D. (1966), Fads, Fashions, and Folderol in Psychology, *American Psychologist*, 21, 343-352.

Dunnette, M.D. and Hough, L.M. (1992), *Handbook of Industrial and Organizational Psychology,* Palo Alto, CA: Consulting Psychologists Press.

Edenborough, R. (2008), Assessment Methods in Recruitment, Selection, and Performance: A Manager's Guide to Psychometric Testing Interviews and Assessment Centres, Milford, CT: Kogan Page.

Furnham, A. and Henderson, M. (1982), The Good, the Bad and the Mad: Response Bias in Self-report Measures, *Personality and Individual Differences, 4,* 519-525.

Goleman, D. (1995), *Emotional Intelligence: Why it Matters more than IQ*, New York, NY: Bantam Books.

Goleman, D. (1998), *Working with Emotional Intelligence,* New York, NY: Bantam Books.

Graves, L.M., Karren, R.J. (1996), The Employee Selection Interview: A Fresh Look at an Old Problem, *Human Resource Management, 35,* 163-180.

Gregory, R.J. (2007), *Psychological Testing: History, Principles, and Applications,* Boston, MA: Allyn and Bacon.

Groth-Marnat, G. (2010), *Handbook of Psychological Assessment,* New York, NY: Wiley.

Guion, R.M. (2010), *Assessment, Measurement and Prediction for Personnel Decisions,* Mahwah, NJ: Lawrence Erlbaum.

Guion, R.M. and Gottier, R.F. (1965), Validity of Personality Measures in Personnel Selection, *Personnel Psychology, 18,* 135-164.

Gunter, B., Furnham, A. and Drakeley, R. (1993), *Bio-data: Biographical Indicators of Business Performance,* London: Routledge.

Hartigan, J.A. and Wigdor, A.K. (1989), *Fairness in Employment Testing: Validity Generalization, Minority Issues, and the General Aptitude Test Battery,* Washington, DC: National Academy Press.

Hogan, R., Hogan, J. and Roberts, B.W. (1996), Personality Measurement and Employment Decisions-Questions and Answers, *American Psychologist, 51*(5), 469-477.

Hogan, T.P. (2007), *Psychological Testing: A Practical Introduction,* New York, NY: Wiley.

Hough, L.M. and Oswald, F.L. (2000), Personnel Selection: Looking Toward the Future–Remembering the Past, *Annual Review of Psychology, 51,* 631-664.

Hough, L.M., Eaton, N.K., Dunnette, M.D., Kamp, J.D. and McCloy, R.A. (1990), Criterion-Related Validities of Personality Constructs and the Effect of Response Distortion on Those Validities, *Journal of Applied Psychology Monograph, 75 (5),* 581-595.

Hunt, S.T. (2008), *The Art and Science of Staffing, Assessment, and Employee Selection,* New York, NY: Wiley.

Judge, T.A., Bono, J.E., Ilies, R. and Gerhardt, M.W. (2002), Personality and Leadership: A Qualitative and Quantitative Review, *Journal of Applied Psychology, 87*(4), 765-780.

Kataoka, H.C., Latham, G.P. and Whyte, G. (1997), The Relative Resistance of the Situational, Patterned Behaviour, and Conventional Structured Interviews to Anchoring Effects, *Human Performance, 10,* 47-63.

Kristof-Brown, A.L., Zimmerman, R.D. and Johnson, E.C. (2005), Consequences of Individual's Fit at Work: A Meta-analysis of Person-job, Person-organization, Person-group and Person-Superior Fit, *Personnel Psychology, 58*(2), 281-342.

Lanyon, R.I. and Goodstein, L.D. (1997), *Personality Assessment* (3rd ed.), New York: Wiley.

Lubinski, D. (1996), Applied Individual Differences Research and its Quantitative Methods, *Psychology, Public Policy, and Law*, 2 (2), 187-203.

Lunenburg, F.C. (2011), The Art and Science of Personnel Selection: The Use of Tests and Performance Simulations, *International Journal of Management, Business and Administration, 15*(1), 1-5.

Mayer, J.D. and Salovey, P. (1997), What is Emotional Intelligence? in P. Salovey and D. Sluyter (eds.), *Emotional Development and Emotional Intelligence: Implications for Educators* (pp. 3-31). New York: Basic Books.

Motowidlo, S.J., Dunnette and M.D., Carter, G.W. (1990), An

Alternative Selection Procedure: The Low Fidelity Simulation, *Journal of Applied Psychology, 75,* 640-647.

Mount, M.K. and Barrick, M.R. (1998), Five Reasons Why the "Big Five" article has been frequently cited, *Personnel Psychology, 51*(4), 849-857.

Mumford, M.D. and Owens W.A. (1987), Methodological Review: Principles, Procedures and Findings in the Application of Background Data Measures, *Applied Psychological Measurement, 11,* 1-31.

Mumford, M.D. and Stokes, G.S. (1992), Developmental Determinants of Individual Action: Theory and Practice in Applying Background Measures, in M.D. Dunnette (ed.), *Handbook of industrial and Organizational Psychology* (2nd ed., Vol. 3, pp. 61-138), Palo Alto, CA: Consulting Psychologists Press.

Murphy, K.R. (2000), Impact of Assessments of Validity Generalization and Situational Specificity on the Science and Practice of Personnel Selection, *International Journal of Selection and Assessment, 8*, 194-206.

Nickels, B.J. (1990), *The Construction of Background Data Measures: Developing Procedures which Optimize, Construct, Content and Criterion-related Validities,* Unpublished doctoral dissertation, Georgia Institute of Technology, Atlanta, GA.

Nickels, B.J. (1994), The Nature of Bio-data, in G. S. Stokes, M.D. Mumford, and W.A. Owens, (eds.), *The Bio-data Handbook: Theory, Research, and Applications* (pp. 1-16), Palo Alto, CA: Consulting Psychologists Press.

Noe, R.A. (2012), *Human Resource Management: Gaining a Competitive Edge,* New York, NY: McGraw-Hill.

Ones, D.S., Viswesvaran, C. and Reiss, A.D. (1996), Role of Social Desirability in Personality Testing for Personnel Selection: The Red Herring, *Journal of Applied Psychology, 81,* 660-679.

Owens, W.A. (1976), Background data, in M.D. Dunnette (ed.), *Handbook of Industrial and Organizational Psychology* (pp. 609-644), Chicago: Rand McNally.

Owens, W.A. and Schoenfeldt, L.F. (1979), Towards a Classification of Persons, *Journal of Applied Psychology, 53,* 569-607.

Paulhus, D.L. (1991), Measurement and Control of Response Bias, in J.P. Robinson, P.R. Shaver, and L.S. Wrightsman (eds.), *Measures of Personality and Social Psychological Attitudes* (pp.

17-59), New York: Academic Press.

Raja, U., Johns, G., and Ntalianis, F. (2004), The Impact of Personality on Psychological Contracts, *Academy of Management Journal*, *47*(3), 350-367.

Robbins, S.P, and Judge, T.A. (2009), *Organizational Behaviour* (13th ed.), Upper Saddle River, NJ: Prentice Hall.

Robbins, S.P. and Judge, T.A. (2011), *Organizational Behaviour* (14th ed.), Upper Saddle River, NJ: Prentice Hall.

Rothstein, H.R., Erwin, F.W., Schmidt, F.L. and Owens, W.A. (1990), Biographical Data in Employment Selection: Can Validities Be Made Generalisable?, *Journal of Applied Psychology, 75* (2), 175-184.

Sackett , P.R. and Lievens, F. (2008), Personnel Selection, *Annual Review of Psychology, 59* (16), 1-32.

Schmidt, F.L. and Rader, M. (1999), Exploring the Boundary Conditions for Interview Validity: Meta-analytic Validity Findings for a New Interview Type, *Personnel Psychology, 52,* 445-464.

Schneider, B. and Schneider, J.L. (1990), Bio-data: An Organisational Focus, in M.D. Mumford, G.S. Stokes and W.A. Owens (eds.), *Bio-data Handbook: Theory, Research and Use of Biographical Information in Selection and Performance Prediction,* Palo Alto, CA: Consulting Psychologists Press.

Tett, R.P., Jackson, D.N. and Rothstein, M.G. (1991), Personality Measures as Predictors of Job Performance: A Meta-analytic Review, *Personnel Psychology, 44,* 703-742.

Thomas, S.L. and Scroggins, W.A. (2006), Psychological Testing in Personnel Selection: Contemporary Issues on Cognitive Ability and Personality Testing, *Journal of Business Enquiry, 5,* 28-38.

Wagner, R.K. and Sternberg R.J. (1985), Practical Intelligence in Real World Pursuits: The Role of Tacit Knowledge, *Journal of Personality and Social Psychology, 49,* 436-458.

Wernimont, P.F. and Campbell, J.P. (1968), Signs, Samples, and Criteria. *Journal of Applied Psychology, 52,* 372-376.

Wigdor, A.K. and Gamer, W.R. (1982), *Ability Testing: Uses, Consequences and Controversies.* Washington, DC: National Academy Press.

5

6 Ps of Talent Retention

Sitanshu Sekhar Das and Byomakesh Debata

Introduction

Talent retention has become one of the most important strategic objectives of organizations of the present time. Talent is essential for survival and is often regarded as a key strategy in maintaining a competitive advantage. Talent retention is needed for success, efficiency, consistency and growth of organization. Talent—what it is, how to acquire it, how to keep it—has become a preoccupation for all the organizations irrespective of their form and nature of operation, because it resides at the heart of growth and competitiveness.

What is Talent?

Executives, researchers, and academicians are talking about talent and put lots of emphasis on talent acquisition, talent management and talent retention. What is that talent? So, far as the dictionary meaning is concerned, talent is a special natural ability; a capacity for achievement or success/ excellence. A few definitions of talent as given by eminent researchers have been given here to make its meaning clearer. According to McKinsey, "talent is the sum of a person's abilities, his/her intrinsic gifts, skills, knowledge, experience, intelligence, judgment, attitude, character and drive. It also includes his or her ability to learn and grow". For McKinsey, talent refers to "the best and the brightest". In the popular book, Top Grading, Bradford Smart (2005) defines talent as, "A players [that] are the top 10 percent of talent available in all salary levels, best of class." Robertson and Abbey also focus on the best and the brightest, in Managing Talented People (2003).

In the views of David Ulrich, talent has three ingredients: competence; commitment; and contribution. (Ulrich, 2006) *Competence* refers to individuals knowledge, skills and values that are required for today and tomorrow; *Commitment* means that employees work hard, put the time in to do what they are asked to do, giving their discretionary energy to the firm's success; and *Contribution* means that they are making a real contribution through their work—finding meaning and purpose in their work. In other words, competence deals with the head (being able), commitment with the hands and feet (being there), contribution with the heart (simply being)". (Ulrich 2006)

Michaels et al. (2001), for example, define talent very broadly as a code for the most effective leaders and managers at all levels who can help a company fulfil its aspirations and drive its performance, managerial talent is some combination of a sharp strategic mind, leadership ability, emotional maturity, communications skills, the ability to attract and inspire other talented people, entrepreneurial instincts, functional skills, and the ability to deliver results.

For Williams (2000), talented people are those who do the following: regularly demonstrate exceptional ability and achievement either over a range of activities and situations, or within a specialized and narrow field of expertise; consistently indicate high competence in areas of activity that strongly suggest transferable, comparable ability in situations where they have yet to be tested and proved to be highly effective.

Phillips and Edwards (2009) defined talent as the employees in critical jobs in an organization—and those jobs are not usually the managers and executives. Critical jobs are important to the success of the organization. Employees in those jobs can make a significant difference in organizational performance.

After reviewing all the above definitions of talent we can conclude that talent is the sum total of all skills, knowledge, experience, intelligence along with the active involvement and effort to take the organization to greater heights of success. So, talent is essential for any organization in order to gain a competitive advantage. After having a clearer understanding of the concept of talent, we must know what is meant by talent retention and why it is important for organization.

What is Talent Retention?

Retention in ordinary sense can be defined as keeping something in possession or keeping engaged in one's service. Here, talent retention simply means keeping the best and bright employees or the talent employees. Talent retention is a process of maintaining long term relationship with the talent employees. It is also defined as a process in which best employees are encouraged to remain with the organization for the maximum period of time. Today, employees have good opportunities in their hand. As soon as they feel dissatisfied with the current employer or the job, they switch over to the next job. Employee retention is more beneficial to the organization than to employees. Therefore, it is the responsibility of the employer to retain their best employees. If they don't, they would be left with no good employees and land nowhere. So, organizations must know how to attract and retain its potential employees.

Why is Retention Important?

Andrew Carnegie once opined: "Take away my people, but leave my factories and soon grass will grow on the factory floors...Take away my factories, but leave my people and soon we will have a new and better factory." This statement of Carnegie though very old, is very true and also hold well today. Employees are very valuable and they can really bring a lot of value and added benefit both tangible and intangible to the organization.

Talent retention is important for the following reasons:

1. Talent retention is important because turnover is expensive. Organizations spend huge time and money on

recruitment, selection and training of employees. Organizations make them corporate ready material. When employees leave the organization immediately after recruitment and training, the organizations do not get any benefit out of investment they make. Recruiting employees consumes a great deal of time and effort. Bringing employees up to speed takes even more time. Various estimates suggest that losing a middle manager costs an organization up to 100 percent of his salary. The loss of a senior executive is even more costly. When the matter is of talent, then definitely it is beyond any cost.

2. Through talent retention organizations maintain a knowledgebase. In the current "Knowledge Era," intellectual capital is what defines a company's competitive edge. Intellectual capital is the unique knowledge and skills that a company's work force possesses. Today's successful businesses win with innovative ideas and top-notch products and services—all of which originate in the knowledge and skills of employees. Talent employees are now considered as intellectual capital, and they are very important for the organization's survival and growth.
3. Talent retention brings stability to the organization and promotes image. When a group of talent employees are retained for a longer period of time, they strongly hold the mission and vision of the organization and act in a sustainable manner and the newer employees are encouraged and build confidence to maintain the healthy working condition. As the retained employees work for longer period of time, they develop an environment of collaboration, which creates a sense of connection through shared experiences, responsibility which ultimately leads to company's success.

The above reasons are enough to substantiate the importance of talent retention for the organizations in the today's competitive world.

The 6 Ps Model of Talent Retention

To retain the talent of employees', organizations must adopt the following purposed model.

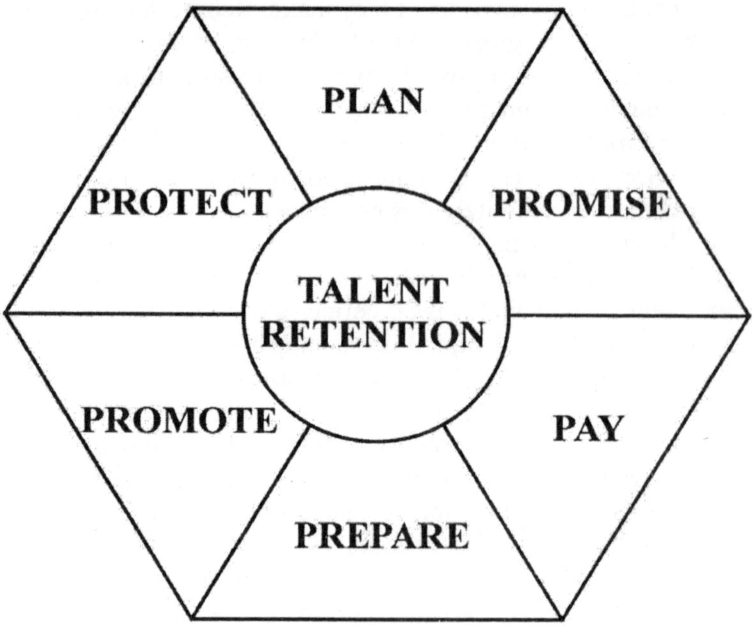

The above model of talent provides that, any organization must go for each of the 6 Ps: plan, promise, pay, prepare, promote and protect in order to retain talent.

Plan refers to the long-term strategy to locate and retain the best and bright performers inside.

Promise not only refers to the assurance made by the organization do everything good for the employees, but also to keep them.

Pay refers to the attractive salary and extra monetary and non-monetary benefits paid to the existing employees and promised to the prospective employees.

Prepare refers to the continual efforts of the organization to train and develop the talent.

Promote again not only refers to the advancement opportunities provided to the employees, but also to the employer branding initiatives which leads to talent retention.

Protect refers to the activities undertaken by the organization to protect the employees against physical and psychological threats, harassment and discrimination.

Let us know more about the each of the 6Ps of talent retention model.

Plan

Without proper planning organizations cannot even attract talents, forget about retention. In order to retain talent, organizations must plan for the same much before they start retaining, because, talent retention is neither an overnight job nor the result of a single strategy. Different strategies are to be adopted to retain the talent employees. Organizations must make strategic plans for locating the talent employees within. Again, there must be detailed planning for rest of the Ps, like what to promise and what not to promise the talent employees so that they will be retained; how to pay and what to pay the talent employees; how to prepare the talent employees so that they will maintain long term relationship with the organization; what to promote and how to promote the employees; and how to protect and against whom to protect the employees every organization who intend to retain their talent employees must plan before hand. After all, organizations must plan about what all they need to do to get the most desired result of retention. So, without a proper plan for everything organizations cannot go for retention. Planning hence, can be considered as the first step towards talent retention. Organizations have to prepare an action plan for the rest of the Ps. The action plans for talent retention must change keeping pace with the changes in business strategy as there may be implications to specific parts of the talent retention strategy. If the action plans for talent retention will not change, then the retention strategy may become antiquated and ineffective.

Promise

Each and every organization makes a lot of promises to allure the employees. Employees are usually attracted by the promises made by the organizations. Most of the promises made include work for an excellent brand, inspirational leadership, commitment to supporting local communities, challenging work, accelerated career growth, continual improvement (personal and professional both), competitive pay, noble mission and values etc. No doubt, these promises and others attract the talents across diversified backgrounds. But, are these promises sufficient to retain the talents? The answer would be "No", because, promises made have no meaning unless and until they are kept rather they will bring discredit to the organization. Making good promises can attract talents, but not keeping the promises may compel them to leave. So, in order to make the organization appear authentic, meritocratic and talent centric organizations must keep all the promises made. Organizations often have to look beyond the concept of satisfaction to developing trust and ensure long term relationships with the employees. Making promises may satisfy the employees but keeping them develops trust among them. Further, this is based on the principle that once trust is built into a relationship, the probability of either party ending the relationship decreases because of high termination costs.

Pay

Every human being is economic by nature. They are primarily motivated by economic incentives and are willing to do things, which maximize their economic returns. Talent employees are not the exception. Excellent employees should not only be given a "reasonable" salary for what they do. They should be paid more than the normal wage since their talent; skills and contribution to the organization are above average. In order to retain employees, organization must reward employees. Rewards present an opportunity to establish your organization as a hard-to-leave workplace—a place people are proud to work in.

Research proves that compensation is one of the largest factors though not the only factor for the retention of employees. Compensation plays significant role in attracting and retaining good employees specially those employees who deliver outstanding performance, and those are considered unique skill and indispensable to the organization because company invested more money on their training and development. Some researchers argue that on the company side competitive compensation package is the only strong commitment and also build strong commitment on the workers side. However, the contribution of compensation towards retention, help in retention of employee irrespective of their skill and contribution to the company and it likely affect turnovers. Most of the time best employees compare their salary with their counterparts in other organizations, and when offered with better package, they switch. In order to avoid this organizations must pay them the best in the industry, so that, employees will not ever compare and think of switching their job.

Finally, employee's stock option plan, special pay, retention pay, gain share pay, performance based pay and bonus etc. seem very small thing, but for the employees they are the prime motivators which helps in retaining the talent employees. Employees' stock option plan enhances the value of the talent employees and maintains a long-term relationship with the talent employees.

Prepare

The organization must prepare the existing talent to lead the organization and face all challenges in the future. Preparation simply refers to the complete process of making the employees corporate ready and updated, by providing all the knowledge skills and abilities required. Stated in other words, prepare refers to the act of training and development.

Research has shown training and development as an important factor in employee satisfaction and motivation. Without training and development a particular job can become stagnant and the employees feel as if they are not advancing. When employees receive additional training, they learn new skills that increase their knowledge and improve their job performance which ultimately leads to their motivation. Also, when an employee is weak in an area, training will help to improve in that area. It also will boost the employee confidence and sense of accomplishment. Training is not just a way to prepare the employees for their day-to-day performance; it is also a way to show them that organizations respect them and want them grow.

Training and development plays key factor in talent retention, because the best employees always hold the urge to update themselves with the latest knowledge and skills available in the market. They want to learn new skills, develop their capabilities, and update their knowledge and advance their careers. If they are not provided with such facilities then they feel de-motivated. In fact, this opportunity for continuous growth and improvement and enhancing knowledge, skills and ability through training and development is one of the most important factors of talent retention. To identify areas of weakness, the organization must use tool such as performance reviews to find out where an employee needs training? A performance review also reveals an employee's ambition where training can help keep the employee who might otherwise go to a new company.

Again training and development not only increases the skills of employees, but also reaffirms to employees that they are valued assets in their organization. They feel good for their organization as they see huge investment in their training and development. This also adds to their satisfaction and motivation which ultimately leads to their retention.

People may question, that why the best people need training and development. Researchers have shown that even the top performers benefits from the training. Training is for everybody. Everybody has the need to learn new and better ways of doing things. Preparation not only ends with the preparation for the work, talent employees need to be trained with the great human skills which will bring them success in their social sphere. Today's organizations are getting more and more diverse so far as their workforce composition is concerned. Consequently, organizations become hot-beds of conflict which may be the reasons of employee turnover. Hence, the managers must be trained to develop and acquire diversity management competencies. So, that they become more tolerant and learn to work with people from diverse backgrounds. These competencies will help them to manage the diverse workforce.

Finally, organizations must prepare the employees for the future vacant jobs through succession planning. Talent successors must be identified and provided with all the requisite knowledge, skills, and abilities to handle the future positions.

Promote

Organizations need to promote their employees. This is one of the proven methods of talent retention. Talent employees may be performing well, but never want to be at the bottom of in the hierarchy. They want an upward movement attached with higher salary and higher respect and higher recognition. The advancement and promotion opportunities lead to employee satisfaction. Promotion should be earned and should be fair, however; seeing others advance unfairly could lead to dissatisfaction. Loyalty, productivity and quality performance are all valid reasons to advance an employee. Opportunity for promotion helps retain employees because they feel that their career and financial future can be improved through their own effort. Promotion lets employees know they are valuable and their organization cares for them.

Promotion not only includes helping people to move in the

job hierarchy, it also means giving them the due respect, recognition and reward that recognition also helps with the retention effort. Praise and recognition are essential to an outstanding workplace. No two employees are equal so far as their performance is concerned; they possess unique strengths, which are why they require recognition of their strengths. Talented employees want to be respected and valued for their contribution. They feel the need to be recognized as an individual or member of a group and to feel a sense of achievement for work well done or even for a valiant effort. They want a 'pat on the back' to make them feel good. Employee recognition is the timely acknowledgement of a person's or team's performance or work behaviour, or business profits.

Recognition and appreciation are the fundamental human needs. Recognition in the form of certificate of appreciation or award of commendation or employee of the month/year award or star performer of the company etc. goes a long way to motivate employees and ultimately leads to their retention. Praising accomplishments of the employees both in terms of large and small; verbally and in writing, promptly and sincerely, publicly and in private motivates them. Employees feel that their good work have been recognized and their work is valued when they receive appreciation from their seniors or authority of the organization. This in enhances their satisfaction and increases productivity. They feel motivated to maintain and improve their performance and their relationship with the organization. Rewards and recognitions are vital for employees' as that have an enduring impact on employees' behaviour and support the perception of employees that they are making a mark in the organization. Similarly, feedback also matter much for employee satisfaction and performance in organization.

Promote also connotes promoting a talent centric culture, which will make the talents feel they are critical to the company success. This talent centric culture also helps in talent retention.

Finally, the organization must promote the self brand image in the market. According to the 2005 Global Workforce Study by Towers Perrin, the single biggest 'driver' resulting in employee satisfaction and consequently employee retention is "reputation of the company as a good employer or employer of choice". One of the main steps in becoming an employer of choice is to let others know about the organization. There are a variety of ways, but the most successful is employer branding. Employees love to be part of those organizations and maintain long-term relationship with organizations which have a very good image in the society. Employees enjoy the job they do in their employer of choice.

Protect

Employees are human beings and they have physiological and security needs. They need protection in terms of physical safety, psychological safety, financial safety and professional safety. The organization which protects the employees against the physical, psychological, financial and professional threats becomes the employers of choice and retains the talent employees. Talent employees tend to maintain long-term relationship with those organizations which provides them financial security now and assure of future benefits in the form of old age pension, unemployment allowance, medical benefit, maternity benefit, gratuity, and provident fund etc.

Second, organizations must provide healthy physical working environment. A safe physical work environment helps in employee retention. (Hytter and Fagerlund, 2008) Employees are motivated to work for such organizations which take care of their health while working by providing them safety equipments like helmet, goggles, gloves, safety shoes water and fire proof clothing etc. They feel good to work for organizations which provide them counselling at the time of need for any reason. Organizations that provide all these protections are better able to retain talent employees.

Third, in order to retain the talented employees, organizations need to create a protected work environment in which employees can work happily. Here, protected work environment connotes a psychological work environment, which consists of work load, deadline, freedom, empowerment, job stress, work climate, relationship with boss, colleagues and others. So, it's the job of the organization to protect talent employees from the fears of deadline, conflict, etc.

Finally, organizations must protect the talented employees from any or all kinds of discriminatory practices and unethical practices which hamper their interest. Employees love to be the part of such organization and maintain long-term association which protects the interest of women, minority groups and persons with disability and persons with diverse backgrounds like age, race, creed, culture and nationality. Organizations which are adopting affirmative action and emphasizing on equal employment opportunities are in a better position to retain diverse talents. In other words, a well managed diverse organization is more able to retain employees than an organization with a homogeneous group of employees. Organizations which break the glass ceiling are the best place to retain women talents. Organizational justice also can go a long way to retain the talented employees.

Conclusion

Talent retention is very important for the organizations of our age as there is a war for talent. Every organization aspires to become successful and gain the competitive advantage over their competitors now a day. To do this organizations obviously need talents who can take the organizations to greater heights of success.

So, talent retention is a main concern for the organizations. The given 6Ps model of talent retention which includes plan, promise, pay, prepare, promote and protect can go a long way to help the organizations to work towards retention of the rarest of the rare talents.

References

Allen, D.G. (2008), Retaining Talent: A Guide to Analyzing and Managing Employee Turnover, SHRM Foundation Effective Practice Guidelines Series.

Barrick, M.R. and Zimmerman, R.D. (2009), Hiring for Retention and Performance, Human Resource Management, Wiley Periodicals, Inc., Vol. 48, No. 2, pp. 183-206,

Cappelli, P. (2008), Talent Management for the Twenty-first Century, Harvard Business Review, March, Vol. 86, Issue 3, pp. 74-81.

CIPD (2009), Talent Management: Factsheet, London, CIPD.

Das, S.S. and Debata, B. (2013), 6Ps Model of Talent Retention, in the R.K. Pradhan and C.K. Podder (eds.), *Human Resources Management in India-Emerging Issues and Challenges,* New Delhi: New Century Publications.

Harvard Business Essentials Series, (2002), Hiring and Keeping the Best People, Harvard Business School Press, Boston, Massachusetts.

Hytter, A. and Fagerlund, S. (2008), Dark Side Leaders, Work Environment and Employee Health, The Dark Side of Organization Conference, Wortley Hall, York University, England.

Marx, M.A. (1995), Keeping Your Best Employees, Journal of Property Management, November, Vol. 60, Issue 6, pp. 26-30.

McKinsey, (2008), How Companies Act on Global Trends: A McKinsey Global Survey", The McKinsey Quarterly Survey on Global Trends, April.

Mendonsa, R. (1998), Keeping Who You Want To Keep: Retaining The Best People, Supervision, January, Vol. 59, Issue 1, pp. 10-13.

Michaels, E., Handfield, J.H. and Beth, A. (2001), The War for Talent, McKinsey and Company Inc.

Phillips, J.J. and Edwards, L. (2009), Managing Talent Retention: An ROI Approach, Pfeiffer, John Wiley and Sons, Inc.

Porter, J.H. (2011), Attract and Retain Top Talent, Strategic Finance, Vol. 92, Issue 12, pp. 56-61.

Ready, D.A. and Conger, J.A. (2007), Make Your Company a Talent Factory, Harvard Business Review, Vol. 85, Issue 6, pp. 68-77.

Ready, D.A., Hill, L.A. and Conger, J.A. (2008), Winning the Race of Talent in Emerging Markets, Harvard Business Review, 86

(11), pp. 62-70.

Srinivasan, M.S. (2011), An Integral Approach to Talent Management, Vilakshan, XIMB Journal of Management, 8(2), pp. 81-90.

Ulrich, D. (2007), The Talent Trifecta, Workforce Management, Vol. 86, Issue 15, pp. 32-33.

Ulrich, D. and Smallwood, N. (2011), What is Talent? The RBL White Paper Series, The RBL Group.

Williams, M.R. (2000), The War for Talent: Getting the best from the Best, CIPD Publishing, London.

Wingfield, B. and Berry, J. (2001), Retaining Your Employees, Thompson Learning, USA.

6

Talent Acquisition, Management and Retention

Sanchali Sinha

Talent Acquisition

Talent can be defined as an individual's ability, aptitude or capacity which is a human capital for an organization. It is marked that with the passing time the demand for talented individual will exceed the availability of talented people with the rising growth of the organization. Getting the right talent as well as retaining the talent for a long time is becoming a challenging job and intensively competitive task for organizations' growth. That is why now-a-days HR professionals are becoming conscious about proper staffing and development. The concept of talent acquisition is nothing but tapping the top performers. Taking the long-term strategic approach to talent acquisition will have a huge impact on how an approach is made to a candidate—if approach is strategic in nature the intent of the call is to go much further, and the conversation becomes more relationship building. Talent acquisition is similar to the acquisition of customers. Thus, by doing proper staffing, recruiting, managing talent within the organization and identification of top performers for further development will help in meeting the challenge of acquiring talent. Hence, the key to talent acquisition is not finding talent but also increasingly, about developing it.

Talent acquisition is the process of recruiting and selecting people and fitting them into the organization as per organization's need. There are various ways/methods which an HR professional can adopt in order to acquire people such as from external sources through advertisements, campus placements, job fairs etc. or through internal sources that is recognizing the required talent or filling the vacancies from the talent existing within the organization. Companies undergo a lot of stress in not only recruiting the people but also in deploying them into their work, proper training, development, planning as the success and the future of the company depends on the quality of manpower they are owning.

Today the traditional recruitment is re-emerging as a broader 'talent acquisition' concept—an approach that is seen to be becoming more and more critical in the 'war for talent'. Talent acquisition forms a broader part of strategic approach in the corporate hunt to gain and sustain a competitive advantage in today's marketplace.

The core concept of talent acquisition is to get away from the 'fill in the box' thinking to one that is more pro-active and much closer to building the skill sets required to achieve business success. Traditionally, a recruitment need occurs when an individual either leaves or is promoted to another function. That's when panic can set in, especially if no suitable internal solution is found, a situation that is becoming known as "under the bus syndrome". Strong relationship building or networking skills are important here. The key to success in talent Acquisition is the unique way that we are able to tap into the 'top performers'. Or say recognizing the next future level or cadre to be vacant in advance and side by side identifying the talent within the organization who can fit into that level and imparting proper training and skills required to them to be a top performer in that respective position. This calls for proper and timely succession planning as well.

Strategic Talent Acquisition

"Strategic talent acquisition goes for a long-term view of not only filling vacancies or positions for today, but also using the candidates that come out of a recruiting campaign as a means to fit into similar positions in the future." These future positions may be identifiable today by doing succession planning, or by analyzing the history of attrition rates for certain positions. This makes it easy to predict that particular openings will occur at a pre-determined period of time.

The strategic approach to talent acquisition has a great impact on how a candidate is being approached. If the approach is made in a tactical way then the question asked to the prospective candidate is regarding his qualification and his interest to join the job. But if the approach is strategic in nature then the conversation goes further as kind of relationship building. The recruiter grabs the opportunity of knowing the candidate's career aspirations, skill sets, interests etc. The recruiter gets to know whether the candidate possesses requisite knowledge and skill set to fit into the position. If the skill set or experience does not match with the current position or requirement; or if the candidate is not prepared for a career move presently, then the candidate can be considered for future prospects. The recruiter has to be in touch with the candidate until either they become available or the candidate gets fit into the required position.

Strategic talent acquisition helps us in creating a pool of competitive talent for present as well as future requirement that would have been missed out. It is just like an addition of small incremental effort, in exchange for a huge potential reward.

Clarify Vision and Strategy: As per the model the talent acquisition process starts with complete understanding and identifying clearly the vision, mission, strategy business model and key issues of an organization by the talent acquisition team. It requires detailed study about the organization's culture so that the talent acquisition strategy adopted is in synchronization with the organization's plans and needs.

Understand Structure and Role Implications: After understanding the vision and strategy of the organization the next step is to review and understand the structure and the role positioning in the organization. It is necessary to understand the type of reporting structure such as whether centralized or decentralized, what are the key variables or key performance areas which the role demands so that based on these factors the talent pool can be created either from external sources or internal sources. This also helps in clarifying the career path and progression of the prospective candidate (new talent) in an organization.

Talent Acquisition Model

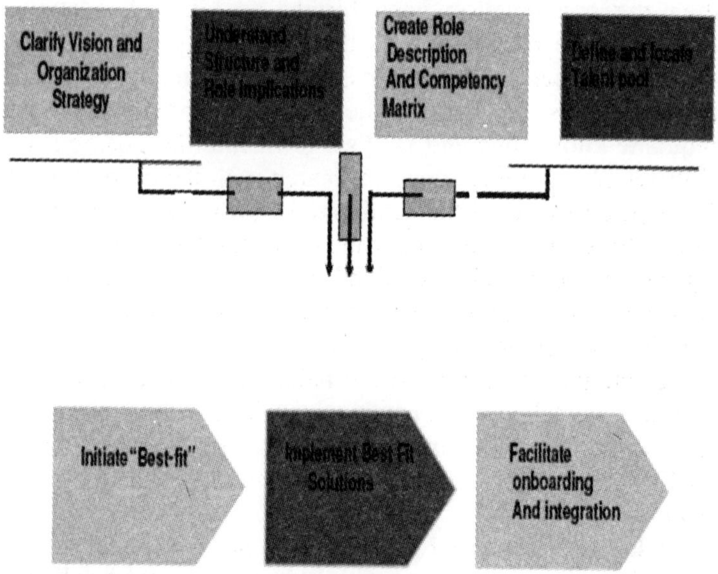

Source: http://www.slideshare.net/shinjinidasgupta/aventus-partners

Create Role Description and Competency Matrix: The study about the structure and role positioning gives an insight into the responsibilities needed to be undertaken for a particular role and the responsibilities handled by the employee in that particular role. This enables in creating the job descriptions for various roles and mapping the competencies required for the roles. The study also helps in indicating the critical incidents which an employee may encounter in his professional life in the organization.

Define and Locate Talent Pool: The above findings are used in acquiring and creating a talent pool having the right combination of skills, knowledge, attitude and other competencies which the role demands.

Initiate Best Fit: The next step is inviting the candidate and providing them a brief knowledge about the role demand, career path and progression, organization's structure so that they can get a fair idea about the role expected from them and helps them in deciding whether they can fit best into the position.

Implement Best Fit Solution: Apart from candidate's understanding regarding their best fit in the role in an organization, the recruiter also takes steps to implement best fit solution. This is done through taking competency based interviews and other skill tests which enables in judging the suitability of the prospective candidate with the organization's need and culture.

Facilitate on Boarding and Integration: This is the final step in the process. After selecting the candidate the next step is facilitating the on boarding process of a candidate in the organization and breaking the barrier or bridging the gap between the candidate and the organization. A proper integration is required between the organization and the new joinees so that the attrition rate at the entry level which is believed to be between 0-6 months is reduced and both the management and the joinees are able to exchange their expectations from each other. This is facilitated by proper induction training and ice-breaking system.

Talent Acquisition Process

Talent recruitment is the process of identifying the prospective employees, stimulating and encouraging them to apply for a job or jobs in an organization. It is a kind of positive action which involves inviting people to apply for a particular position in an organization. The purpose of recruitment is to create an inventory of eligible/talented persons from amongst whom proper selection and placement of the right person at the right job can be made.

There are two dimensions of the recruitment process. One is that in all cases recruitment involves locating and attracting adequate human resources to fill existing vacancies and the other is that recruitment is a critical management activity. The right people are the future of the organization. No organization can survive in the absence of human resources. So recruiting the best talent and making them fit into the right job in the organization is a challenge for every recruiter in an organization.

Preparation for Recruitment

Before starting the process of inviting people for the job there is a need to decide what kind of persons are needed and what should be their characteristics. This calls for fixing the 'job specifications' which is based on 'job description' which describes the nature of the job. Thus, job specification and job description will be different for every job. The various elements of job specification are as follows:

1. **Physical Specifications:** For certain jobs, some special physical features may be required. For example, for assembly of a TV set or some other electronic equipment good vision is required, for a typing job you need finger dexterity, for a heavy job you need a strong, heavy and thick-set body. The particular physical abilities and skills necessary for a given job have to be specified. These may refer to height, weight, vision, finger dexterity, voice, poise, hand and foot coordination, motor coordination, colour discrimination, age-range, etc.
2. **Mental Specifications:** These include intelligence, memory, judgment, ability to plan, ability to estimate, to read, to write, to think and concentrate, scientific faculties, arithmetical abilities, etc. Different jobs require different degrees of such abilities and the more important ones

should be specified.

3. **Emotional and Social Specifications:** These include characteristics which will affect his working with others, like personal appearance, manners, emotional stability, aggressiveness or submissiveness, extroversion or introversion, leadership cooperativeness, initiative and drive, skill in dealing with others, social adaptability, etc.
4. **Behavioural Specifications:** Certain management personnel at higher levels of management are expected to behave in a particular manner. These are not formally listed but have to be kept in mind during the process of recruitment, selection and placement.

Sources of Manpower (Recruitment)

There are two categories of sources of supply of manpower-internal and external.

1. **Internal Sources:** These include personnel already on the pay-roll of the organization as also those who were once on the pay-roll of the company but who plan to return, or whom the company would like to rehire.
2. **External Sources**: These include sources from outside the organization, like the new entrant to the labour force without experience. These include college students, the unemployed with a wider range of skills and abilities, the retired experienced persons.

There are many advantages in accepting manpower from within the organization, i.e. recruiting from internal sources as employees are already accustomed with the organization culture, need less training/induction, and more over it improves the morale of the employees and improves loyalty among them towards the organization. However, there are some disadvantages also as it would lead in discouraging new breed from entering an organization. This would restrict an organization from getting new talent, new skills, new competencies etc. Moreover a new talent can bring new ideas in the organization. However, recruiting from external sources has also got some demerits as the organization has to take chances regarding the loyalty and desire to continue for the person selected under this system and at the same time the investment on training is also high for a new entrant.

Methods of Recruitment

A. Direct Methods: Direct methods include recruitment from educational and professional institutions, employee contacts' with public, manned exhibits and waiting lists.

1. **Schools and Colleges:** Candidates are taken from schools and colleges and other professional institutions which usually have a placement officer or a teacher-in-charge of placement, who normally provides help in attracting employers arranging interviews, furnishing space and other facilities and providing student resumes. The companies maintain a list of such institutions, keep in touch with them, send their brochures indicating job openings, future prospects, etc. On the basis of these, students who want to be considered for the given job(s) are referred to the company recruiter.
2. **Employees' Contacts with the Public:** The organization brings into the knowledge of their employees about the existing vacancies so that they can bring candidates from their own referral such as friends, relatives etc. which is also known as employee referral program.
3. **Manned Exhibits:** The organizations send recruiters to conventions and seminars, setting up exhibits at fairs in order to get the desired candidate.
4. **Waiting Lists:** Many firms lean heavily on their own application files or resume bank. These records list individuals who have indicated their interest in jobs, either after, visiting the organization's employment office or making enquiries by mail or phone. Such records prove a very useful source if they are kept up-to-date.

B. Indirect Methods: Various types of indirect methods include advertising in newspapers, on the radio, in trade and professional journals, technical journals and brochures. When qualified and experienced persons are not available through other sources, candidates are invited through advertising in newspapers and professional and technical journals. A well thought-out and planned advertisement for an appointment reduces the possibility of unqualified people applying. If the advertisement is clear and to the point, candidates can assess their abilities and suitability for the position and only those who possess the requisite qualifications will apply. An advertisement should be clear about the job description and job specification so that unqualified candidates do not apply and becomes easy for the recruiter to select.

C. Third-Party Methods: Under this method, various agencies are used for recruitment. Some of the agencies are described below:

1. **Private Employment Agencies**: These agencies deals in specific occupation like general office help, salesmen, technical workers, accountants, computer staff, engineers and executives, etc. The objective of these agencies is to understand the need of the organization and to bring together the employers and suitable candidate available for the required job.
2. **State or Public Employment Agencies**: These are the main agencies for public employment and are also known as Employment or Labour Exchanges. They also provide a wide range of services, like counselling, assistance in getting jobs, information about the labour market, labour and wage rates, etc.
3. **Executive Search Agencies:** Complete information and records about executive personnel are maintained by these agencies. They provide job opportunities for higher cadre to the candidate. These agencies are often termed as 'head hunters', 'raiders', and 'pirates'.
4. **Indoctrination Seminars for College Professors**: These are arranged by the companies where professors are invited and the problems of the company are discussed

with them. These are done so that professors get impressed and later in the future requirements they can speak well about the company and help them in getting the right personnel.

5. **Friends and Relatives of Present Employees**: This is another source of getting manpower. But the problem with this method is that it is likely to encourage nepotism which may create problem for the organization.
6. **Trade Unions:** Under this method, trade unions are often called on by the employers to help them in hunting for suitable candidate. Unions may be asked for recommendations largely as a matter of courtesy, goodwill and cooperation.
7. **Temporary Help Agencies:** These agencies employ their own labour force, both full-time and part-time and make them available to their client organisations for temporary needs.
8. **Casual Labour Source:** These are the one which present themselves daily at the factory gate or employment office. Most industrial units rely to some extent on this source. This source is the most uncertain of all sources.

Selection Procedure

1. **Initial Screening or Preliminary Interview:** This a preliminary stage in which the applicants are given necessary information about the nature of the particular job as well as information is being taken from the applicant about their experience, knowledge, skills, expected salary etc. If there is a match found between the candidate's expectations and the organization's requirement then the candidate is given an application form to fill in. This process is usually carried out by the junior level executives in the organization.
2. **Application Scrutiny:** In this stage the applicant is asked to furnish details about his age, marital status, educational qualifications, work experience and references.

Organization may use different application form for different employees e.g. one for managers, one for supervisors etc. Some forms are simple, general and easily answerable, while others ' may require elaborate, complex and detailed information. An application form should be designed in a way so that it serves as a highly effective preliminary screening device.

3. **Selection Tests:** After scrutinizing the application form the next step is to go for a selection test as it is not possible for the organization to allow every applicant for the interview as the number of applicants always exceeds the number of vacant posts.

A test is a sample of an aspect of an individual's performance, behaviour or attitude. It is a kind of systematic procedure for comparing the behaviour of two or more persons.

1. **Purpose of Tests:** The basic assumption underlying the use of tests in personnel selection is that individuals are different in their job-related abilities and skills and that these skills can be adequately and accurately measured.
2. **Types of Tests**: The various tests used in selection can be put into four categories: (a) achievement or intelligence tests, (b) aptitude or potential ability tests, (c) personality tests, and (d) interest tests.

A. Achievement or Intelligence Tests: These are also termed as 'proficiency tests'. These tests are used to measure the skills or knowledge which is learnt as a result of a training programme and on the job experience. These are of two types:

1. **Test for Measuring Job Knowledge**: These tests are also termed as 'trade tests'. These tests are used to understand the knowledge of a candidate on some machines, equipments, typing etc. Oral tests consisting of series of questions are administered to the candidate in order to judge whether the candidate has got a thorough knowledge on trade or occupation.

2. **Work Sample Tests:** These tests help in measuring the proficiency level of the candidate in the work. This is done by giving the candidate a work to do and measuring the accuracy, effectiveness and time taken by the candidate in completing the work.

B. Aptitude or Potential Ability Tests: These tests are used to measure the potential capacity, aptitude of a candidate. This helps to judge the intellectual capacity of a person as well focuses on particular type of talent such as learning, reasoning etc. These tests are of following types:

1. **Mental Tests:** These tests measure the overall intellectual ability or the intelligence quotient (IQ) of a person and enable to know whether he has the mental capacity to deal with new problems. These determine an employee's fluency in language, memory, induction, reasoning, speed of perception; and spatial visualization.
2. **Mechanical Aptitude Tests:** This is used to measure the capacity of a person to learn a particular type of mechanical work. These are useful in the selection of apprentices, mechanics, maintenance workers, and mechanical technicians.
3. **Psychomotor or Skill Tests:** These measure a person's capacity to do a specific job. These are administered to judge the mental dexterity or motor ability. These are primarily used in the selection of workers who have to perform semi-skilled and repetitive jobs, like assembly work, packing, testing, inspection and so on.

C. Personality Tests: These discover clues to an individual's value system, his emotional reactions, maturity and his characteristic mood. The tests help in assessing a person's motivation, his ability to adjust himself to the stresses of everyday life and his capacity for interpersonal relations and for projecting an impressive image of himself. They are expressed in terms of the relative significance of such traits of a person as self confidence, ambition, tact, emotional control, optimism, decisiveness, sociability, conformity, objectivity, patience, fear, distrust, initiative, judgment, dominance, impulsiveness, sympathy, integrity, and stability. These tests are given to predict potential performance and success for supervisory or managerial jobs. Personality tests are used to know the characteristics or traits of a person such as his ability to adjust to the organization's culture, stress, leadership quality, self confidence, emotional control, interests, patience, impulsiveness, motivation, stability, ambition etc. These tests are administered to predict the potential performance and success for managerial or supervisory positions.

The personality tests are of three types:

1. **Objective Tests:** These measure neurotic tendencies, self-sufficiency, dominance, submission and self-confidence.
2. **Projective Tests:** In these tests, a candidate is asked to project his own interpretation onto certain standard stimuli. The way in which he responds to these stimuli depends on his own values, motives and personality.
3. **Situation Tests:** These measure an applicant's reaction when he is placed in a peculiar situation, his ability to undergo stress and his demonstration of ingenuity under pressure. These tests usually relate to a leaderless group situation, in which some problems are posed to a group and its members are asked to reach some conclusions without the help of a leader.

D. Interest Tests: These tests are designed to understand a person's areas of interest and to identify the kind of work that will satisfy him. Questionnaires are projected to the candidate and the answers provided by the candidates are analyzed to know their area of interest in doing the job.

Limitations of Selection Tests: All the above tests described do not provide a hundred percent guarantee that a person selected on the basis of the above test will definitely prove to be an efficient employee. This tests are used and implemented only on the basis of assumption that a candidate securing more than cut off marks in the tests will be comparatively a better prospect as compared to the person securing less than the cut off marks. However, tests will serve the purpose only when they are properly constructed and administered.

Precautions in Using Selection Tests: Test results can help in selecting the best candidates if the following precautions are taken:

1. Norms should be developed as a source of reference on all tests used in selection and on a representative sample of people on a given job in the same organization. This is necessary even though 'standard' tests are available now under each of the above categories. Norms developed elsewhere should not be blindly used because companies differ in their requirements, culture, organization structure and philosophy.
2. Tests should first be validated for a given organization and then administered for selection of personnel to the organization.
3. Each test used should be assigned a weightage in the selection.
4. Test scoring, administration and interpretation should be done by persons having technical competence and training in testing.

Interview: Meaning and Purpose

An interview is defined as a conversation between two parties i.e. an interviewer and interviewee with a purpose of: (i) obtaining information, (ii) giving information, and (iii) motivation. It should provide an appraisal of personality by obtaining relevant information about the prospective employee's background, training work history, education and interests. The candidate should be given information about the company, the specific job and the personnel policies. It should also help in establishing a friendly relationship between the employer and the applicant and motivate the satisfactory applicant to want to work for the company or organization.

Types of Interview:

1. **Informal Interview:** This may take place anywhere. The employer or a manager in the personnel department may ask a few questions, like name, place of birth, previous experience, etc. It is not planned and is used widely when the labour market is tight and you need workers very badly. A friend or a relative of the employer may take a candidate to the house of the employer or manager where this type of interview may be conducted. This kind of interview usually takes place when the labour market is very tight and it becomes very difficult for an organization to attract the talent from the market or from other competing organization. In such case employer may take interview anywhere casually and may ask a few questions, like name, place of birth, previous experience, etc.
2. **Formal Interview:** This is a well structured interview which takes place with all formal process in the organization in the stipulated place and time.
3. **Planned Interview:** This is also a kind of formal interview which is carefully planned. The interviewer sets a plan of action in relation to time to be devoted to each candidate, type of information to be sought, information to be given, the modality of interview and so on.
4. **Patterned Interview:** This is also a planned interview but planned to a higher degree of accuracy, precision and exactitude. A list of questions and areas is carefully prepared. The interviewer goes down the list of questions, asking them one after another.
5. **Non-directive Interview:** This is a kind of unstructured interview and is designed in a way to let the interviewee speak his mind freely. The interviewer is a careful and patient listener, prodding whenever the candidate is silent. The motive behind this kind of interview is to give the candidate a chance to 'sell' himself without encumbrances of the interviewer's questions.
6. **Depth Interview:** The objective of this interview is to

intensively examine the candidate's background and thinking and to know in detail the interest of candidate on a particular area. The idea behind it is that if the candidate is found good in his area of special interest, the chances are high that if he is given a job in his area of interest then he would be interested and efficient in doing that job.

7. **Stress Interview:** This interview is used to judge the candidate's capacity to handle and manage stress by creating a situation of stress and strain. This test helps in analyzing the person's behaviour in a stressful situation.
8. **Group Interview**: In this type of interview group of people are brought together and given a topic of discussion. These kind of interview is used to judge how an individual behave and adjust with each other, how they present their views against each other, way of leading the topic, participation ad reaction on each others views.
9. **Panel Interview:** This kind of interview is conducted by members of the interview board or a selection committee. This is undertaken for selecting candidate for supervisory and managerial positions. It pools the collective judgment and wisdom of members of the panel.

Limitations of Interviews:

1. One prominent characteristic of a candidate may be allowed to dominate appraisal of the entire personality.
2. The interviewer's experience may have created a close association between some particular trait and a distinctive type of personality.
3. Subjective judgment of the interviewer may be based on his prejudices, likes, dislikes, biases, etc.
4. Some managers believe that they are good at character analysis based on some pseudo scientific methods and are guided by their own abilities at it.

Qualities of 'Good' Interviewers:

A good interviewer should have the following qualities:

1. Knowledge of the job or other things with which interviews are concerned.

2. Sensitivity to the interviewee's feelings and a sympathetic attitude.
3. Extrovert behaviour and considerable physical and mental stamina.
4. Emotional maturity and a stable personality.

Guidelines for Improving Interviews

Not all interviews are effective. Their effectiveness can be improved if the following points are kept in mind by an interviewer:

1. An interview should have a definite time schedule with ample time for interview. It should not be hurried.
2. Interview should have the necessary element of privacy.
3. The impersonal approach should be avoided.
4. Attention should be paid not just to the words spoken, but also to the facial expressions and mannerisms of the interviewee.
5. The interviewer should listen carefully to what the applicant says and the information collected should be carefully recorded either while the interview is, going on or immediately thereafter.
6. The interviewee should be told where he stands—whether he will be contacted later, whether he is to visit another person, or it appears that the organization will not he able to use his abilities.
7. The interview should end when sufficient information has been gathered.
8. Reference checks and final decision.
9. Placement .Sometimes a particular person is selected for a given job. Often more than one person may be selected for the jobs of similar nature. In the second case, individual employees have to be put under individual supervisors with the approval of the latter. In the first case also his approval is also necessary but it should be done early in the selection process.

   A proper placement helps in reducing employee turnover,

absenteeism and accident rates and improves morale.

Induction, Orientation or Indoctrination

This is the last process after selecting the candidate i.e. induction or orientation programme. It is a kind of formal introduction of an employee to the job and the organization's people. The primary purpose is to 'sell' the company to the new employee so that he may feel proud of his association with the company and to make them feel as a part of the company and make them comfortable. This helps a new entrant to know his fellow workers, and also policies and practices of the organization. A proper induction program helps in reducing attrition rate at the entry level and absenteeism.

A good induction programme should cover the following:

1. The significance of the job with all necessary information about it, including job training and job hazards.
2. The company, its history and products, process of production and major operations involved in his job.
3. Employees own department and job, and how he fits into the organization.
4. Personnel policy and sources of information.
5. Structure of the organization and the functions of various departments.
6. Terms and conditions of service, amenities and welfare facilities.
7. Company policies, practices, objectives and regulations.
8. Grievances procedure and discipline handling.
9. Rules and regulations governing hours of work and overtime, safety and accident prevention, holidays and vacations, methods of reporting, tardiness and absenteeism.
10. Opportunities, promotions, transfer, suggestion schemes and job satisfaction.
11. Social benefits and recreation services.

An induction programme consists primarily of three steps:

1. **General Orientation by the Staff:** This kind of

orientation provides necessary general information about the history and the operations of the firm. This helps an employee in building up some pride and interest in the organization.

2. **Specific Orientation by the Job Supervisor:** In these the employee is given complete knowledge about his department and work, about the practices and customs of the organization. This helps an employee to adjust with his work and environment.
3. **Follow-up Orientation by either the Personnel Department or the Supervisor:** This kind of orientation is conducted within one week to six months of the initial induction and by a specialist or by a supervisor. The purpose is to find out whether the employee is reasonably well satisfied and confident enough to start work with the induction programme. Personal talks, guidance and counselling efforts are made to remove the difficulties experienced by the new entrant.

Talent Management

Management of talent refers to providing proper development, training, compensations and incentives to the employees. The management of talent is very important in order to ensure that the people are always in a position to give their best to the organization. Proper talent management is making the judicial use of resources. The talent management takes care of the development of the individuals in the organization and develops them in order to fulfil the current as well as future needs. It ensures their proper growth and promotion within the organization as well as also ensures that the turnover rate is as low as possible and the available workforce is suited for all needs.

Talent management requires that HR professionals and the organization understands how they define talent, who they regard as 'the talented people' and what their typical background might be. Talent can be seen as a complex amalgam of employees' skills, knowledge, potential and cognitive ability. Employees' values and work preferences are also of major importance.

Now how to identify and measure all these attributes is a challenging task with a number of issues arising. For example, whether it is possible to develop a profile of what to look for when trying to recruit and select 'high flyers'—those with potential to take the position of senior management or professional roles. Understanding the motivational factors for high performers, one should assess the talent and manage them. It is sometimes critical to understand which technique to be used in order to assess them and which kind of training needed to be imparted to them in order to help them learn more and develop and maintain their talent.

There are some questions which arise when undertaking a talent management program. For example, whether talent management should be focused exclusively on an elite subgroup of future leaders of the organization or at least those capable of progressing through a number of steps .The 'exclusive' mode of talent management is characterized by a concentration on those in one or two segments (or talent 'pools') of the workforce who are either at the top or who are identified as having the potential to get to the top by demonstrating high levels of potential or performance. If operating in this mode, there needs to be clarity about what it is that makes 'an exceptional manager' (Delbridge et al. 2006, p. 141), i.e. one who can make a strategic difference.

However, some commentators have expressed concerns about strategies that concentrate exclusively on an elite high-potential, rather than those that take a more inclusive 'whole workforce' approach. A more 'inclusive' approach is necessary, they argue, because '...an inclusive talent management strategy is a competitive necessity'. (Chris Bones cited in Warren, 2006, p. 25)

But this is not an easy endeavour as different organizations recognizes different forms of inclusivity. Some organizations, apart from capitalizing on those identified as having the potentiality to be the future managers, also considers professional staff, technical experts and knowledge workers.

Irrespective of different approaches adopted by the organizations, it is necessary to pay attention by the organization regarding the needs of the organization to face the current and forecasted future challenges and linking those challenges and needs to the performance, development, motivation and reward needs of the employee.

Need for Talent Management

Costs: The cost of replacing an employee with scarce skills is considerably high. Some talent is not available easily in the labour market in that case recruitment cost also rises while attracting such expensive talent from the labour market which is scare. So organization must try not to loose such talent to other hands.

Risk: Despite of adopting various techniques and methods for recruitment and selection of the best talent it is found that all those techniques cannot provide a guarantee that a talented employee will not leave the organization. Some people leave the organization as they could not fit into the organization's culture or value systems. In order to avoid the risk of losing talented resources the organization calls for an effective talent management program.

Client Service and Opportunity Costs: When an organization looses a talented resource, it not only enters into the risk and cost of hunting another talented resource but also the services provided by the organization to its clients or say customers also gets hampered as there is sometimes a long gap between a vacancy created and a vacancy filled up especially in case of scare talent. Sometimes the organization has to compromise future business with the associated opportunity costs.

Lack of Capacity: Lack of people with suitable skills and talent is a key restraint in terms of service capacity. This manifests itself at 2 levels. Firstly, a firm soon reaches a state of over pressure. Some of the consequences faced by the firm are deadlines are missed, reduced standards and quality of work. The firm fails or lacks the capacity of managing growth or managing ups and downs associated with the business. Secondly, the firm becomes so consumed with meeting operational deadlines that it loses its ability to keep itself up to date with latest best practice, legislation or other issues demanding new skills. In this case clients will soon recognize that mistakes are made due to lack of currency of skills. These are some of the more visible risks to firms who do not pay attention to the attraction, growth and retention of key talent. Beyond the visible, other manifestations of the problem arise. Staff morale declines because leadership talent is absent and this energy drop is transferred to the client. Internal politics and protection of territory or unwillingness to share information and surface problems affect the functioning of the firm. All of these things affect the ability of the organization to offer great service and take advantage of opportunities to grow.

Challenges in Talent Management

Attracting/Recruiting Talent: Attracting and recruiting talent with high professional, technical and leadership quality is the biggest challenge posed on an organization in the competitive international and local labour markets. The problem arises specially when recruiting for higher managerial posts with up to date knowledge and skills.

Rewarding Talented Recruits: Creating a motivational reward structure is another challenge faced by the organization in managing their talent. Traditional system of rewards and incentives schemes may not prove to be attractive to the new generation. An organization need to tailor its reward system as per the attitude and value system of an individual. For example, one day extra pay may not be a motivational reward factor for a supervisor but the same may means a lot to a lower level employee say attainder of the organization.

Other considerations might be:

1. How should rewarding for potential versus rewarding for performance be addressed?
2. How can the rewarding of talent be aligned with other reward systems?
3. How is reward segmented (for example, with regard to potential senior managers and specialists with core skills)?

Organizing Groups of Talent: 'Banks' and 'Pools': Organizing talent banks and pools is a challenged faced now a day by the organization with growing competition in attracting the best talent from the market. Many organizations go for recruiting talent when a vacancy is created while many organizations build their talent banks and pools before or after recruitment. Talent banks operate where an organization identifies and attracts potential candidate before they're required, as candidates often emerge who are clearly desirable and interested in joining the organization but there may not be a suitable current vacancy. By periodically being in touch with these candidates and informing them when appropriate opportunities arise, companies save time and expense in future searches.

Talent pool is the name given to a collection of talented employees once they've joined the organization. While creating a talent pool it is required to decide about the kind of talent pools that should exist, processes for identifying employees for an internal talent pool, tools to identify those employees' skills and how to 'map' the skills to the needs of the organization at a certain place at a certain time.

Diversity of Talent: An organization faces the challenge of managing diversity at work. This diversity compromises of diversity in business i.e. how much an employer is progressing and its ability to recruit and retain the best talent. It refers to the ability of an organization in building talent across the organization and ensuring equality of opportunity in the work force. Another aspect is the diversity of thinking i.e. a challenge for an organization to recruit a talent which can think 'out of the box'. Delbridge et al. (2006, p. 232) suggests that, 'Mavericks who flout all rules can rarely achieve the centrality within the network of relationships among key organizational members that they need for pursuing significant initiatives. The challenge is to conform to some rules in order to earn the legitimacy and credibility to break others.' This focus on building the capability of the individual requires employees on a talent management programme and their managers to engage in regular, constructive 'conversations'.

Appraising Talent: Appraisal involves measuring or checking the actual results achieved by employees' against the standards set within those areas where they are held accountable and to examine the level of skills or competencies deemed critical to current and future jobs and organizational success. In relation to a talent management programme, certain specific areas are important. For example, the appraisal will not only include an examination of performance, but will also inevitably include a forecast of potential, which is a prediction of how many job levels an employee can reach within the organization based on their past or current performance approaches, training or development needs, career preferences and actual and projected competency levels. Here, scales are often used in reporting potential to attain managerial or leadership skills, as well as in the delivery of organizational objectives (for example, 5 = greatly exceeds expectations, and 1 = greatly below expectations). These may change over time, depending on the pace and success of development of the individual, and a number of organizations report gathering human capital metrics on this progress.

However, care must be taken about the nature of the development and who is chosen to be developed as 'talent'. For example:

1. Consideration should be given to the choice and alignment of different learning and development interventions, such as management training and coaching/mentoring.
2. Budgets can be badly spent because of the lack of focus on

the development 'rewards' that are given to people in talent pools.

3. How does talent management link to any career planning processes in place? A number of organizations encourage employees to take responsibility for their career management, which can induce a 'sink or swim' policy where only the very strong survive. This might not be the best policy for employees requiring additional support, such as those operating in a different geographical, technical or cultural domain as part of their developmental processes.
4. Offering an insufficient range of development programmes can produce too wide a separation between 'those who have talent' and 'those who don't', many naturally talented employees not being developed and employee resentment occurring.
5. Potential leaders can be provided with strategic-level experience but not enough experience of operational management tasks.
6. Leaders can be developed who are superficially skilled but not committed to the organization.
7. How do you talent manage employees who show different levels of potential at different stages of their careers?
8. Line managers need to be adequately informed about the aims and objectives of a talent management initiative and provided with training in important areas such as coaching.
9. How do you work with those employees who show potential but are not motivated to be developed/develop themselves?
10. It is clear that leaders are informally developed as well as formally. Networking and building social capital and trust comes into the equation with informal processes. There are therefore questions about how and why this process comes about, in what circumstances, and so on.

Training and Developing High Potential Individuals

It is required to understand that the challenge faced by the organization do not ends with talent acquisition and retention and managing through various techniques. An organization need to train and develop even its high potential employees and help them in unblocking their talent. An employee needs to be trained in the way of applying its talent practically at work. They need to develop in the areas such as emotional intelligence, technical skills, and the ability to perform beyond their potential zones by acquiring and learning new skills and potentials. Some of the in house talent management program can be coaching, mentoring, succession planning.

Deploying Talent: Deployment places an important role in talent management and job rotation and job enrichment are vital aspects of experiential learning in becoming a leader. New recruits with high potential joining an organization could well have expectations that they'll be required to be mobile and therefore to move around the organization. If this doesn't happen, it can lead to employee engagement and commitment problems later on. So an organization should take care of deploying talent properly at work, roles and responsibilities which is in alignment with the individual's talent.

Tracking Talent: In order to have any measure of success, talent management needs to be informed by accurate reporting to identify where talented employees came from and how successfully they're being deployed. Tracking talent therefore involves recording and analysing human capital data on the movement of key employees through the pipeline over time and their current and future value to the organisation. This requires good-quality human capital metrics, such as internal promotion rates, which can be used to better align talent management techniques and strategies.

Retention of Talent: Retention of talent forms an important feature of talent management which is often overlooked by an organization. All kind of recruitment and selection technique, deployment, training, rewards goes in vain if a talent leaves an organization. Today's challenge for an organization is how to manage talent in a way to retain them long in the organization. It is important to check the employee turnover because although an organization needs 'new blood' to join with more modern and new sets of skills and talent but also it requires key talent to stay. However, very few organizations show interests in maintaining account of key talent leaving the organization. Those who can maintain contact with leavers, especially in the first month when they might feel they've made the wrong decision and would happily return to their 'old' organization if there was a re-establishment of terms and conditions, such as rewards would be helpful for the organization.

Organizations are made up of human capital i.e. people: people creating value through proven business processes, innovation, customer service, sales, and many other important activities. As an organization struggles to meet its business goals, it must make sure that it has an integrated and continuous process for recruiting, training, managing, supporting, and compensating these people. The above shows the complete process which are described below:

1. **Workforce Planning:** The first step starts with workforce planning. There should be integration between the business plan and the plan for workforce such as hiring plans, compensation budgets for the year, training plans etc.
2. **Recruiting:** After planning for workforce, recruitment begins. There should be proper co-ordination between the staffs of the organization while recruiting so that right talent gets an entry into the organization.
3. **On-boarding:** It is the prime responsibility of an organization to provide proper induction and knowledge about the organization and work to the new joinees.
4. **Performance Management:** By referring the business plan, the organization establishes processes to measure and manage employees.
5. **Training and Performance Support:** It is the duty of an organization to provide training to the employees and support them to learn and develop new skills and talent at work.

Talent Management Process

Source: Bersin and Associates (2006), Performance Management 2006; The Fast Growing Market for Workforce Performance and Talent Management Solutions.

6. **Succession Planning:** As the organization expands and changes, there is a continuous need to shift people into new positions. Succession planning is a very important function which enables managers and individuals to identify the right candidates for a position when a vacancy is created. Succession planning also needs to be aligned with the business plan in order to understand and meet requirements for key positions. While this process is often

used for managers and executives, but it is more commonly applied across the organizations.

7. **Compensation and Benefits:** This is an integral part of people management. Here, organizations try to link the compensation plan directly to performance management so that compensation, incentives, and benefits are in alignment with business goals and business execution.
8. **Critical Skills Gap Analysis:** This process is being identified as an important process but often overlooked function in many industries and organizations. Often there lies a gap between the skills or competencies required to do a job in the organization and the skills or competencies possessed by an individual. If the gap sustains it will affect the business of the organization in terms of quality, service rendered etc. So, it calls for mapping proper job description, job specification and competency mapping for each and every job so that based on these, the gap can be identified and proper learning and training could be provided to the employee in order to bridge the gap.

Talent Retention

Today the main concern for any organization (whether small or large; private, public or non-profit) is its ability and framing strategy to attract, engage, and retain the right people in the organization. The main problem of retention is the scarcity of talent with relevant work skills for today's jobs, the changing work values and the high cost of turnover. Some of the strategy or processes which will help an organization to retain its talent are discussed below:

Selection: A proper recruitment and selection method and hiring the right person is a start up point for retention. For this an assessment of basic job skills and an examination of the "softer" issues such as motivation, values, and being able to fit into the organization are also important. This factor tends to have a powerful impact on employees' success and tenure with a company.

Professional Growth and Development: Training and development opportunities act as an incentive for many employees to stay with a company. This is true especially when an employee is concerned about his career growth and tailors its development plan that meets their particular goals.

Meaningful Work and Ownership: An employee needs to know that whether he is making a difference and being effective in his jobs. An organization should clearly define to their employees regarding their expectations and responsibilities. Employees need to understand how their roles are linked to the organization's overall success. Employees should be given that work which matches their skills and knowledge as well their expectations from the organization, as an employee who is involved in determining how work gets done have a sense of ownership and an opportunity to contribute to improvements and success in the company's performance and remains associated with the company for a longer period of time.

Developing an Attractive Employee Value Proposition: An employee value proposition means that the particular company has something attractive to offer as compared to other company that is perceived as valuable to an employee. An employer needs to understand that what makes his organization attractive to potential candidates and current employees. Branding yourself as an employer of choice is not just a slick set of marketing tactics. The best advocates for an employer's brand are its current employees or say their word of mouth. It is important to know what messages the existing employees send to others about their employer. Are they honestly saying and believing that, "This is a great place to work." This issue provides a great insight into the retention strategy.

Create a Total Reward Structure that Includes More than Compensation: Every company should have all the normal compensation mechanisms common to their type of employment. Yet, total rewards packages go far beyond money. While money might temporarily retain employees, it does not always equate with engagement. People want a chance to make a difference and realize themselves. That self-realization is multi-dimensional and different for each employee, the total reward structure should include, in addition to compensation, support for employees to attain their personal objectives aligned with the goals of their organization.

Give Feedback on Employee Performance on a Regular Basis: Now a days companies are very tactful about measuring performance of an employee with proper performance appraisal system as they follow knowledge linked pay system. An appraisal process helps in judging employee's performance and providing them correct feedback.

Periodic feedback on performance allows employees to know better about where they stand in the organization, and gives them a formal means to provide input, indicates that their managers pay attention to them and that their performance matters. This feedback contributes to employee engagement and retention.

Be Flexible in Terms of Work-Life Balance: Employees value a balance between work and life. They want to have flexibility in the organization and want to engage with their employer in a flexible way. To attract and retain workers with different work and career expectations, organizations have to be more flexible in structuring work and its expectations. It calls for a different managerial mindset and practices that involve flexibility in the ways of controlling workers' time and attendance but without affecting the business.

Creating a Culture of Engagement: Employees have become more connected with others in the organization (and the broader supply-and-customer chain) through project-based team work and process management activities. Employees are shifting their loyalty to people, teams and projects and away from company loyalty. It is organizations that create the culture and climate that allow people, processes and projects to become fully connected and engaged with one another.

Engaged employees are more likely to stay with their employer.

Train Managers to be Effective: An analysis of exit interviews will reveal that "poor and bad" management practices greatly contribute to an employee's decision to leave a company. It is imperative to provide supervisors and managers with adequate tools to become effective managers since we cannot assume that these competencies are innate.

There are many reasons why workforce attrition is such a vital concern:

1. The cost of churn—recruiting, hiring, and time-to-productivity—is steep, especially for highly professional staff.
2. Loss of key players affects corporate productivity.
3. The cost of vacancy, particularly at peak periods, can negatively impact shareholder value.
4. Loss of top talent to a competitor can lessen competitive advantage.
5. Frequent staff changes and new, inexperienced employees cause customer dissatisfaction.
6. High attrition affects morale of the remaining workforce.

Conclusion

Quick and frequent changes of the external environment make higher and higher demands on organizations. For every organizations the main asset to manage those changes are people. In the absence of a skilled workforce, without employees equipped by required abilities and knowledge, organizations will not be able to keep up with competition and even may not be able to survive under specified conditions.

Human resource planning is the pillar of talent management system which ensures the right availability of talents. In order to link the human resource activities with the organizational goals, workforce planning is a must. It helps in bridging the gap between the current and the required human resource. Managing talent equally plays an important role as that of managing finance in an organization. In the era of talent, where there is the best come best serve basis, every company should make sure that it is able to attract the best talent and that is why there is also race among recruiters to grab the best of the lot when there is a scarcity of talent in the labour market. The talent acquisition process is incomplete without the management, development and retention of talent. The talent development is a two dimensional in the way that it is beneficial for the company as well as the employees. The importance of acquiring talent, providing training and developing them, managing the talent and undertaking measures to retain them can be well understood from the simple fact that companies incur one-third of their cost for workforce management.

References

Brown, J.S. and Duguid, P. (1991), Organizational Learning and Communities-of-Practice: Toward a Unified View of Working, Learning, and Innovation. Organization Science 2(1), 40-57.

Berger, L.A. and Berger, D.R. (2004), *The Talent Management Handbook*. New York: McGraw-Hill.

Horvathova, P. and Mikušová, M. (2011), Acquisition of Talents from Organization's Internal Sources, *2010 International Conference on Business and Economics Research*, Vol. 1, pp. 5-8.

Khatri, P., Gupta, S., Gulati, K. and Chauhan, S. (2010), Talent Management in HR, *Journal of Management and Strategy*, 1 (1), pp. 39-44.

Mathur, R. (2010), Talent Acquisition: A Challenge for Human Resource Professionals, *Lachoo Management Journal*, 1(1), pp. 103-108.

http://www.academia.edu.

http://www.cipd.co.uk/NR/rdonlyres/6101AA06-F0C7-4073-98DA-758E91C718FC/0/3832Talentmanagement.pdf.

http://www.bf.umich.edu/docs/KeyReferenceArticles.pdf.

http://www.willamette.edu/mba/faculty/B2B_Claus.pdf.

http://www.avatarresources.com/main/images/stories/Docs/Employee_Retention.pdf.

7

Workforce Diversity: A Study of Selected IT Companies

Lopamudra Hati and Madhusmita Panda

Introduction

A diverse workforce is a reflection of a changing world and market place. Diverse work teams bring high value to organizations. Respecting individual differences will benefit the workplace by creating a competitive edge and increasing work productivity.

Managing diversity is one of the most important challenges faced by managers and their organizations. In today's work environment, co-workers are likely to be of different gender, age, religion, cultural background, race and ethnicity. They also differ in terms of lifestyle, choices available, perspectives, attitudes, value system, beliefs, behaviours, expectations, skills and experiences. These issues are not just about discriminatory practices but they modify the nature and demands placed on leadership and management and bring into prominence the concept of diversity.

How managers are well prepared to invest in the concept of diversity will impact not just on work issues but also on sensitivity to customer's needs, legal compliance, business' ethical issues, profitability and even social cohesion. Diversity management is a strategic process to manage a diverse workforce—including the fight against stereotypes, prejudice and all kind of discrimination due to the individual perceptions and assumptions—in the manner to maximize the benefit and minimize barriers of different opinions, behaviour and attitudes of human beings within a company.

Accenture

"Diversity is essential to our ability to deliver high performance to clients. Our global workforce gives clients access to a rich range of talent, representing different styles, perspectives and experiences. This diversity is a critical strength that we work hard to maintain and foster. It makes us a better company on every dimension". (Pierre Nanterme, Chief Executive Officer)

"Accenture is passionately committed to cultivating a diverse workforce both because it's the right thing to do, and it's a key element of achieving high performance," Armelle Carminati-Rabasse. (Accenture MD of Human Capital and Diversity)

"We know the markets we serve are growing increasingly diverse and we are proud of how diversity management has become part of our day-to-day business practices," Clyde Jones (Chief Diversity Officer).

Accenture comprises people from a wide range of cultural, educational and geographic backgrounds–people who are able to challenge conventional thought, offer unique perspectives and generate innovative ideas. In an independent study commissioned by Accenture on cross-cultural communication problems, it was found that the chief factors causing problems between onshore and offshore workers were different communication styles (76 percent of the times), different approaches to completing talks (53 percent), different attitudes toward conflict (44 percent) and different decision-making styles (44 percent). In Accenture the diversity management include 3 approaches, these are:

1. Accenture inclusion and diversity culture.
2. Accenture programmes.
3. Women.

1. Inclusion and Diversity Culture: In February 2003, Accenture formally established a Global Inclusion and Diversity corporate function to provide strategic guidance and support for Accenture's diversity programs and activities in countries around the world, and to promote a discrimination-free and harassment-free work environment for all employees.

A. Accenture's Geographic Human Capital and Diversity Organization: In each of Accenture's geographies, an executive serves as human capital and diversity geographic lead. The executive creates programs that are valuable to employees, and clients around the world. There are two additional governance bodies, the members of these bodies demonstrate shows their passion for diversity and complement the work of this team:

- **Accenture Diversity Council:** The Accenture Diversity Council, which includes members of their Global Management Committee, assesses the inclusion and diversity challenges we face, sets strategic direction and prioritizes our actions globally.
- **Diversity Advisory Forum:** The Diversity Advisory Forum, a group of senior executives representing its global locations, provides the Accenture Diversity Council with additional perspective from the field and recommends innovative, groundbreaking solutions to inclusion and diversity challenges.

2. Accenture Programmes: It conducts program either at a global level or from within its geographies, help to build an inclusive culture.

A. Cross-Cultural Programs: Accenture serves clients in more than 120 countries around the world. It provides online and classroom training for people at all levels that is aimed at heightening employees' awareness of cultural differences. It also offers a wealth of resources and robust tools that build awareness and acceptance of the personal styles and values of others.

One such resource is Globe Smart, which offers 24/7 online access to up-to-date information on global business effectiveness. Additionally, Accenture people have access to training, such as an online Building Cross-Cultural Awareness course, which teaches participants how to maximize value with a multicultural team.

B. Employee Resource Groups (ERGs): In many cities around the world, Accenture supports groups, meetings and other opportunities to connect individuals who wish to strengthen their support network. ERGs help to build connections and address issues that are of interest to them personally. These groups, which may be organized around a common interest, ethnicity, sexual orientation, career path, family arrangement, faith or religion, focus on an individual's needs and interests, as well as the needs of the communities in which they work and live.

ERGs are based on local demand and interest, and differ from location to location. No matter where they are, their goals are to:

- Promote diversity through initiatives that focus on education, awareness, professional and personal development and cross-cultural interactions.
- Foster a means for individuals with similar backgrounds to network around similar challenges and opportunities.
- Offer professional direction.
- Support national and local recruiting and retention efforts.
- Build external relationships with diverse businesses.
- Support diverse non-profit organizations as part of our corporate citizenship initiative.

For example, employees in the United Kingdom have access to interest groups ranging from ethnicity to enablement for people with disabilities, to sexual orientation and religion.

C. Flexible Work: At the individual level, flexibility enables Accenture to attract, retain and engage its diverse workforce. Flexibility is important for managing a corporation by integrating principles of inclusion into practice and enabling Accenture to effectively perform and compete in the global business market. Accenture nurtures a culture of work-life balance with equal emphasis on work and personal life by integrating principles of inclusion into practice. The global and country-specific flexibility policies show the specific work arrangements that are formally considered "flexible work." They are as follows:

- Part-time.
- Job sharing.
- Flex-time.
- Telecommuting/working from home.
- Engagement programs: full weekends at home.
- Extended weekends at home: extended client/home location.

D. Persons with Disabilities: Accenture is committed to creating and providing an inclusive, open and equitable environment for individuals with different backgrounds, lifestyles, needs and expectations to be successful. In order to build awareness and understanding of issues faced by persons with disabilities, it sponsors networking and information sharing and encourages the provision of reasonable accommodations - modifications or adjustments to a job or the work environment to assure that a qualified individual with a disability has rights and privileges in employment equal to those of employees without disabilities—to create an adaptable work environment.

Its geographic units and countries have developed a variety of initiatives specifically to support persons with disabilities. For example, the Mobile Café, a road shop business run by persons with disabilities, recently debuted in Seoul with support from Accenture in Korea. The coffee-shop-on-wheels were formally presented in October 2010 by Accenture Korea to the Korea Rehabilitation Fund (KRF), a non-profit organization that provides professional barista training to persons with disabilities. Accenture's volunteers assisted in the planning and execution of Skills to Succeed initiative, which will provide persons with disabilities skills and employment opportunities to become active members of society.

E. Training: Training is a priority in Accenture's overall career experience, and is one of the most effective ways we can make inclusion and diversity part of our culture. Accenture offers training programs to educate individuals, to promote inclusion and diversity in the workplace and to prepare our people to deliver high performance through a diverse workforce.

We embed diversity topics into many of our core curriculum courses and also offer stand-alone diversity training. The variety of courses Accenture offers, educates and inspires our people, develops our diverse workforce, and enables our people to foster an inclusive environment.

Accenture divides inclusion and diversity training into three areas:

- Diversity awareness to help develop a greater sensitivity to the challenges and opportunities presented by working in an increasingly dynamic, global and diverse organization.
- Diversity management to help our leaders more effectively manage a diverse workforce and create an inclusive work environment.
- Professional development to help solidify the integrated approach to deepening our commitment to our women and minorities by helping build skills to increase their personal success in Accenture.

F. Supplier Diversity: Accenture believes that diverse suppliers should have equal opportunity to participate in the procurement sourcing process. It focuses not only on expanding own pool of diverse suppliers, but also encourage its large suppliers to leverage diverse suppliers on Accenture's behalf.

G. The Diverse Supplier Development Program: In 2006 it launched a formal mentoring program between Accenture executives and diverse suppliers, the diverse supplier development program (DSDP). The eighteen month program comprises quarterly training symposia—on topics such as business development and sales effectiveness, strategic planning, marketing, cloud computing and environmental sustainability to name a few—and one-on-one meetings between Accenture executives and partnered suppliers, who learn more about our business and strategies to expand their businesses. The meetings, tailored for each individual based on the needs of the supplier with the expertise of the mentor, provide participants with an opportunity to learn about and discuss topics that they have identified as key challenges in running and growing their businesses, as well as to network and seek counsel from Accenture executives.

H. Transgender Network: It is committed to raising awareness and educating all Accenture people about its LGBT (lesbian, gay, bisexual and transgender) community, while simultaneously supporting its LGBT employees and providing a workplace of equality. In 2010, Accenture became one of only nine companies in the United States to implement Transgender Transition Guidelines that comply with World Professional Association for Transgender Health standards.

On a global basis, Accenture has:

- Included sexual orientation and gender identity and expression of language in its non-discrimination policy.
- Made provision for same-sex domestic partners with accompanied cross-border assignment benefits and a global medical plan for long-term assignments and some transfers benefits.
- Supported local LGBT Network teams.
- Legalalised policies to ensure the equal treatment of employees, regardless of sexual orientation or gender identity.
- Imparted training on inclusiveness of bisexual and gender identity issues.

3. Women: From the training and mentoring programs, to celebration of International Women's Day, to internal networks connecting women around the world with each other and with available resources, Accenture is committed to supporting women.

Tata Consultancy Services (TCS)

"The DNA of the company is to create an easy work

environment and this has been built over years of effort".

–*S. Ramadorai* (Vice Chairman, TCS)

"We want people to retain their identity yet be integrated into the company currently, 7.5 percent of our workforce consists of non-Indians,"

–*Mr. S. Padmanabhan* (Executive VP and Head-Global HR)

TCS is an equal-opportunity employer. TCS has the culture of celebrating everything under the sun, singing carols at Christmas and doing the "Dandiya" dance at "Navrathri" with equal enthusiasm.

TCS believes work force diversity can be managed properly through 2 ways:

- Leaders and managers must create a strategic plan to develop diversity initiatives throughout the organization.
- Leaders and managers within organizations must incorporate diversity policies into every aspect of the organization's functions and purpose.

Employees' Views and Involvement is Key to the Success of Diversity Initiatives: Organizations must view employee participation as a necessary part of the diversity initiative, in order to develop and maintain effective diversity policies. The leaders of the best practices organizations understand that they must support their employees in learning how to effectively interact with and manage people in a diverse workplace. They recognize that they should encourage employees to continue to learn new skills in dealing with and managing people. They also recognize the impact that diverse clients will have upon the success or failure of an organization, as businesses must compete to satisfy these clients.

A diverse organization is shaped or influenced by the basic corporate culture, which comes from the vision and mission of the founder-promoter. Then there's the influence of the geographical culture. The company is largely influenced by the personal culture of the people at the mid-management and senior management levels. Then, surprisingly, it is also shaped by the client culture. Outlining some of the challenges for companies opting for an increasingly diverse and global workforce, Kalyanaraman (Senior Manager) said that as workers are increasingly relocating and migration is on the rise, organizations need to devise retention strategies with "a passionate focus on individual, team and geo-wise expectation charts." He recommends that companies should conduct a deep study of issues such as worldwide compensation and aspiration benchmarks. "No two countries have the same retirement benefits," said Padmanabhan of TCS.

Infosys

"We firmly believe that the future success of Infosys lies in its ability to create an environment that is open to people from different nationalities and ethnicities".

–*S. Gopalakrishnan*, CEO, Infosys

"Talent is imperative in today's economy and the increase in globalization means the competition for global talent is rife. At Infosys, we recognize the importance to invest in skills globally and provide opportunity for future business leaders to understand the changing dynamics of a flat world".

–*N.R. Narayana Murthy*, Chairman and Chief Mentor, Infosys

Infosys recognizes and promotes this power of diversity to drive innovation. Infosys strives to employ people representing the widest possible variety of nationalities, cultures, genders and gender identities, sexual orientations, employment histories, and levels of physical ability. In doing so, the company is able to recruit new employees from all available global talent pools and provide paths to employment to all members of world societies, including talented individuals from groups who may have in the past been under represented within the IT industry. Within such a diverse company, people bring to the workplace contrasting opinions and worldviews. As these people interact, they develop new ideas, methods, and perspectives.

Infosys actively fosters inclusivity across all of its business units and in every one of its company offices. It encourages all employees to focus on the commonalities they share and leverage their differences towards productive teamwork. Inclusivity ultimately makes for a more informed and sensitive employee base that is better able to serve clients.

Infosys was the first Indian IT company to establish a company office to manage and drive all company initiatives dealing with diversity and inclusion. Today they have employees from over 83 countries. Women constitute more than 33 percent of their workforce. Infosys Women Inclusivity Network (IWIN) encourages and nurtures a gender-sensitive work environment. IWIN recognizes the aspirations and needs of women. It provides opportunities for vocational, personal and psychological counsel to ensure professional and personal growth. Its new Family Matters Network provides ample support to its employees on the matters of effective parenting.

Infosys received the first NASSCOM-India Today corporate award for excellence in gender inclusivity in 2007. Infosys actively seeks to hire and train persons with disabilities. In 2006 and 2007, Infosys BPO received the Helen Keller award for the best employer from the National Centre for Promotion of Employment for Disabled People (NCPEDP).

Infosys declared an intake of 300 graduates from universities in the US in 2006 and about 25 from universities in the UK in 2007 as part of its commitment to create a diversified workforce. The new employees will develop their engineering skills at Infosys development centres across India for six months before returning to Infosys offices in the US. Infosys has a global workforce with more than 91,000 employees from 70 nationalities working in 90 countries. As a recruitment strategy, Infosys hires graduates from universities worldwide and trains them at its Global Education Centre, Mysore. The first batch of students from the United Kingdom was inducted in 2007. Infosys is practicing this model across countries to develop a world-class workforce.

Infosys BPO Bags Excellence Award for Diversity Hiring Initiatives: For 2009 INFOSYS BPO, the business process outsourcing subsidiary of Infosys technologies, has received the ASTD Excellence in Practice Award for its diversity hiring initiatives. This prestigious award honours a practice which leverages diversity for enhanced performance, and recognizes corporate programs or efforts to address issues around intercultural, gender or sexual orientation. Infosys BPO is the only company to be honoured under this category. The awards were evaluated in nine categories such as learning technologies, valuing differences, organizational learning, workplace learning and development amongst others. Infosys BPO currently employs 208 people with disabilities.

To consistently take business growth to the next level and beyond, Infosys has following approaches to manage diversity.

Promote Diversity in Leadership Positions: This practice provides visibility and realizes the benefits of diversity in the workplace.

Embrace Diversity: Successfully valuing diversity starts with accepting the principle of multiculturalism. Accept the value of diversity for its own sake—not simply because you have to. You need to reflect your acceptance in all you say and do.

Recruit Broadly: When you have job openings, work to get a diverse applicant pool. Avoid relying on referrals from current employees, since this tends to produce candidates similar to your present workforce.

Select Fairly: Make sure your selection process doesn't discriminate. Particularly, ensure that selection tests are job-related.

Train all Employees: Encourage all employees to embrace diversity. Provide diversity training to help all employees see the value in diversity.

Strive to be Flexible: Part of valuing diversity is recognizing that different groups have different needs and values. Be flexible in accommodating employee requests.

Wipro

Wipro launched of its Women of Wipro (WoW) initiative, coinciding with the international Women's Day. Wipro honoured its women workforce with the title of 'Green Ambassadors' besides felicitating women achievers. The Wow initiative has been launched as a chapter of the Wipro's Diversity Council, as the company's Green Ambassadors will influence a change in the environment by undertaking various projects that emphasize on the aspect of 'Green' The initiative will be driven by the Green Ambassadors at a personal level. WoW will also work towards creating visibility for its female leadership, both internally and externally.

Building sustainable and growing networks that contribute to the success of business, the community and self-development would be the other highlight of initiative. Wipro Chairman Azim Premji said, "In corporate India, I have been seeing very positive shifts in the last few decades that have made it easier for women to contribute to organizational growth. There are many instances where the so-called glass ceiling has been shattered. There is no doubt that having more women in an organization can help in making it more profitable. "Eco Bags specially made for women employees were given away on the occasion. The 'Eco-Bag' contains quick and easy list of green steps, called "Shades of Green". Going forward, the WoW charter will include several initiatives that have a significant social impact and where women can play a catalytic role in ushering change. The Core Diversity Council has been set up to breathe life into these initiatives so that they don't remain buried in a Power Point presentation. The council consists of representatives from every function at a senior level.

Conclusion

We are born differently at different times, under different circumstances, at different places by different parents and so we are different. As this is true for people in the entire world, it is very true for subsets of the world such as the organizations. Employees in any organization vary in all aspects of their being. Diversity not only involves how people perceive themselves, but how they perceive others. . Managing diversity in organizations absolutely dependent upon the acceptance of some primary objectives to which employees are willing to commit, such as the survival of the firm. In today's fast-paced work environment a successful organization is one where diversity is the norm and not the exception.

References

Jain, H.C. and Verma, A. (1996), Workforce Diversity, Employment Equity/ Affirmative Action Programs and Public Policy in Selected Countries, *International Journal of Manpower,* 17(4/5), 16-29.

Richard, O. (2000), Racial Diversity, Business Strategy and Firm Performance: A Resource-based View, *Academy of Management Journal*, 43, 164-177.

Thomas, D.A. (2004), Diversity as a Strategy, *Harvard Business Review*, 82(9), 98-108.

Vedpuriswar, A.V. (2008), The Power of Differences, *Indian Management*, 47(1), January: 76-83.

Werner, J.M. and Desimone, R.L. (2006), *Human Resource Development,* Cengage Learning, pp. 352-364.

http://www.accenture.com/us-en/company/people/diversity/Pages/index.aspx

http://www.accenture.com/us-en/company/people/diversity/Pages/diversityculture.aspx

www.careers.tcs.com

http://www.infosys.com/newsroom/infosys-in-the-news/Pages/diverse-workplace.aspx

http://www.infosys.com/sustainability/diversity/pages/index.aspx

http://www.infosys.com/newsroom/press-releases/Pages/diversity-hiring-award.aspx

http://www.infosys.com/about/awards/Pages/gender-inclusive-practices.aspx

www.tcs.com/news_events/analyst_reports

http://www.mahindra.com/Careers/Life-at-Mahindra/Diversity

www.tcsemployment.com

http://www.wipro.com/insights/general-research/

8

A Proposed Talent Management Architecture

Atri Sengupta and Arun K. Sinha

Introduction

Talent management has drawn the maximum attention of strategy-makers in the corporate world both in India and abroad. Indian industries are no exception to this. Based on a survey of CEOs of 114 leading companies across diverse sectors, Moster.com reported that 73 percent of Indian CEOs spend over one-fourth of their time directly on talent related activities. (21st June, 2011, Economic Times) One of the roles of CEOs is emerging as chief talent officer. Creating talent pools, strategic hiring, developing, retaining and managing talent are the key area of responsibilities of the chief executives. According to a BTI study, 60-70 percent of Indian CEOs spend their time on talent recruitment and retention. (28th June, 2011, Economic Times) Reason behind this is the alarming scenario of talent shortage worldwide.

Talent is the most precious resource for the organization to stand in competition. But growing talent shortage creates bottle-necks to the strategic moves of the organization. It is being difficult for the employers to identify right talent for their organizational requirements to face the emerging business challenges. Based on a survey of 1396 human resource practitioners from over 60 countries, Deloitte (2005) reported that attracting and retaining talent are the two most critical issues faced by the organisations. In the post-recessional period with around 8 percent GDP growth in 2011-12 in India, although the rate is lower than the last fiscal year, every industry is currently witnessing an upward rising business growth curve, and hence, planning for aggressive business expansion. Talent is undoubtedly the key imperative for the organisations to stand in the volatile business situation and cut throat competition.

However, talent reality shows the paucity of high-performing talent, thus putting organizations into talent war. To win the battle, they even prefer to adopt unfair practices, such as, poaching or lateral hiring. A report is showing that Maruti-Suzuki, India's largest automobile company is into the trap between talent shortage in labour market and talent poaching by its rivals like Volkswagen, Honda, BMW, Audi and Hyundai which are offering fatter salaries to lure high performers away from the Delhi-based car maker. To deal with the problem mentioned, Maruti is now planning to induct its young professionals for senior management positions.

However, this is to be noted here that for the immediate gain, majority of the organizations, unlike some big corporate giants viz. Hindustan Unilever, Infosys, etc., are more concerned about lateral hiring than talent development. Several talent management strategies are taken by the organisations and thus different talent management models are getting evolved. Surprisingly, different organisations are having different definitions and understanding about talent. Some prefer to define all their employees in the organisation as talent; some indicate towards star performers of the organisations; and some explain talent as attributes which are quite similar to human competencies. This results in utter confusion about what talent is or how is it different from the terminologies like human resource, human capital, or competency. Present article aims at: (i) operationalising 'talent' by critically evaluating existing literatures, and (ii) proposing a new talent management model for organisational success.

Conceptualizing Talent

What is Talent? It is the talent which provides competitive edge to the organisation from rest of the players in the business segment. Talent has been an integral part of business in the journey from industrial era to knowledge era, thus proved itself most precious resource of the organisation. Strategy-makers are now focusing on how to align talent with business strategy so as to earn competitive edge. How to attract, develop and retain talents in the organisation are the major focuses of any talent management model. Talent war, talent crisis, talent strategies, talent management department are the common words in organisational dictionaries. But unfortunately no such dictionary is there which defines talent objectively. Definition of talent varies across jobs, organisations and industries. This lack of consensus to operationalise talent is, perhaps, making the talent management concept more confused and complicated. It is needless to mention that an effective talent management model begins with defining talent properly.

Talent is an age-old term having a range of meanings from "a denomination of weight" to "according to his ability", "capital", "inclination or disposition", "treasure, riches, mental endowment, and natural ability", "special natural ability or aptitudes and faculties of various kinds", and "embodied in the talented–hence, a person of talent and ability". (Tansley, 2011, p. 267) Oxford Reference English Dictionary–Indian Edition (2008) defined talent as "a special aptitude or faculty" or "high mental ability"; whereas Longman Dictionary of Contemporary English (2006) defined it as "a natural ability to do something well". Thus, it can be said that talent is a special natural ability which has got some worth. According to Gladwell (2010), "talent is equal to ten years or 10,000 hours invested in a specific field". Talents are very few in numbers who have the ability to excel or create difference (Sloboda, 1985; Gagne, 2000) in a particular field.

Not everybody is talented for a specific purpose. Those natural abilities of an individual should be considered as 'talent' which create benefits for him or her and for others in a particular situation. Talent is very much purpose specific. For example, an employee might have singing ability which is not adding value to the organisational growth, cannot be considered as 'talent' for the organisation. But the same singing ability can be considered as 'talent' for any art and cultural organisation. This is to be noted here that the natural abilities which are not getting exposed or used for a purpose cannot be considered as 'talent'. Even, a specific talent may no longer be a talent for an individual, if, not practised within a period. Thus, talent has got an expiry feature.

Is Talent Innate or Learned?

A debate continues amongst the researchers whether talent is innate or learnt. Some authors are in favour of conceptualising talent as 'in-born' or 'gifted' quality, for example, talent in sports (Tranckle and Cushion, 2006) or education. (Heller et al., 2000) However, many are in support of 'learnt' feature of talent. Gagne (2000) argued that talents are the capabilities of an individual which make differences and those capabilities are the result of individual's learning experience. Barab and Plucker (2002) also believed that talent emerge because of training and education. These definitions create more confusion between talent, competencies, skills, etc. Linguistically, talent means 'natural ability' which indicates towards inherent nature of the term. Transley (2011, p. 268) stated "an innate quality or ability is one that you were born with, not one you have learned". Many other authors in different languages are also in the same tune. For example, in Danish language, Politikens (2000) viewed talent as "innate abilities"; Ozehov (1984) in Russian explained it as "outstanding innate qualities, especially natural gifts".

These arguments raise the debate of talent is an outcome of nature or nurture. Simonton (1999) viewed talent is the outcome of both nature and nurture. Thus, talent can be said as innate ability (Echols, 2007) of a person in a particular field that can create excellence or make difference from others. They excel with ease and grace. A talented person has a certain aura in their ability that others wish to emulate and from which lesser mortals draw inspiration". Does it mean talent is not required to be learned? It should be noted here that talent is innate ability which is required to be sharpened or nurtured. It cannot be emerged just out of training and education. Learning or training is useful then when the ability is innate in nature. Otherwise these are more applicable to skills or competencies which are not inherent so as to talent.

Talent versus Competencies versus Skills

Many authors included competencies as a part of talent. For example, Michaels et al. (2001, p. xii) conceptualised talent as "the sum of a person's abilities–his or her intrinsic gifts, skills, knowledge, experience, intelligence, judgment, attitude, character and drive. In addition, it includes his or her ability to learn and grow". The definition unnecessarily broadens the boundary of the concept of 'talent'. All abilities of an individual can not be considered as natural which can drive excellence. Talent are equally very few in number as the talented persons are. An individual may learn many competencies in the course of his life time. However, all of them cannot be termed as 'talent'. For example, an employee has many competencies, but amongst those, on a very few he has real mastery or extraordinary performance and his/her passion is visible for those. These can be termed as 'talent'. Skills, on the other hand, are the application of technical knowledge in a particular field.

Talent=innate ability to create excellence, getting nurtured and practiced.

Skills=application of technical knowledge in a particular field.

Competency=sum of knowledge, skills, attitudes and abilities.

Talent in Organisations

The idea of some organisations, in this regard, to define

their entire workforce as 'talent' for their organisations and accordingly strategize talent management is really questionable. Everybody in the organisation cannot be talented so as to add value to its competitive edge. Talent is available to a limited pool of organisational members. (Ready et al., 2010) Glastra and Meerman (2012) viewed talent as the term fits with what organisation or the managers, the talent-scouts, look for. Talent, sometimes, is viewed as not an individual trait, but an outcome of systematic interactions between employees and selective agents within the work organisations. (Barab and Plucker, 2002) It should be noted here that talent is an innate ability of an individual and it can be nurtured through the systematic interactions between employees and selective agents within the work organisations, but it cannot be emerged out of these interactions.

Based on the discussion mentioned above, 'talent' can be operationalised as the natural and innate ability of an individual in a specific field which has the capacity to drive excellence in a said purpose. Talent can be nurtured through proper training, learning, and practice, however, without these it will expire within a span of time. Talent can be made visible either through individual's passion for his/her said ability, or by the nurturing leaders of the organisation.

Talent Management Architecture

Several talent management models have been evolved so far. Some researchers focused on talent development structure (Glastra and Meerman, 2012; Garavan et al., 2012), some integrated talent and knowledge of the organisations (Whelan and Carcary, 2011), some explains it in terms of talent acquisition, development, retention, performance management, succession management etc. (Romans and Lardner, 2005; Heinen and O'Neill, 2004; Scheweyer, 2004; Lewis and Heckman, 2006) Talent management can be said as the architecture which helps the organisation to systematically identify and channelize talents for the competitive edge in current and future business challenges. Each organisation is having its own set of requirements to reach competitive edge and talent can be segmented accordingly.

The present talent management architecture has aligned three phases–business strategy-making phase, talent function and HR functions. Talent function has further been divided into three phases. Firstly, talent pool which can be defined as the collection of talents available in the organisation or in the market. Assessment centre, mentoring can be the processes to identify talents from within the organisation and employer branding can be the strategy to attract talents from outside the organisation. This can also be helpful for retaining talents. Talent identification is the most important phase of the talent function.

This phase is aligned with effective hiring of HR functions. In the second phase of the talent function, talent segmentation and talent pipeline are developed. Segmenting talents as per the organisational requirements, current and future, includes different perspectives of the talents which are taken from talent pool, such as, innovation, leadership, problem-solving, decision-making, achievement-oriented, etc, which are the drivers of organisational excellence. Talent pipeline, on the other hand, is a channel of talents availability. This focuses on nurturing of talents, developing talent facilitating culture, etc. Succession planning, career management or learning and development of HR functions play important role here. Last phase of the talent function makes sure how talent can drive as well as deliver organisational excellence, thus, aligned with performance management systems, reward policy of HR functions.

Conclusion

To conclude, defining 'talent' is the most important part of any talent management model. Unnecessarily broadening the concept by including HR aspects has made the term confusing with current existing knowledge of competency, HRM, skills, etc. Present article attempted to operationalise 'talent' objectively and proposed a Talent Management Architecture by aligning talent function with business strategy and HR functions.

References

Barab, S.A. and Plucker, J.A. (2002), Smart People or Smart Contexts? Cognition, Ability, and Talent Development in an Age of Situated Approaches to Knowing and Learning, *Educational Psychologist,* Vol. 37, No. 3, pp. 165-82.

Chartered Institute of Personnel and Development (2007), *Talent Management: Strategy, Policy, Practice,* Chartered Institute of Personnel and Development, London.

Deloitte (2005), *Becoming a Magnet for Talent: Global Talent Pulse Survey Results*, Canadian edition, available at: www.deloitte.com/dtt/research/0,1015,cid percent253D103148,00.html, April 3, 2007.

Echols, M.E. (2007), Learning's Role in Talent Management, *Chief Learning Officer,* Vol. 6, No. 10, pp. 36-40.

Economic Times (21st June, 2011), *CEOs Spend More Time on Talent Management Activities, says survey,* PTI.

Economic Times (28th June, 2011), *Talent Management Tops Company CEOs' Task List*, Devina Sengupta and Writankar Mukherjee, ET Bureau.

Gagne′, F. (2000), Understanding the Complete Choreography of Talent Development through DMGT-based Analysis, in Heller, K.A., Monks, F.J., Subotnik, R.F. and Sternberg, R.J. (eds.), *International Handbook of Giftedness and Talent*, Elsevier Science, Oxford.

Garavan, T.N., Carbery, R. and Rock, A. (2012), Mapping Talent Development: Definition, Scope and Architecture, *European Journal of Training and Development,* Vol. 36, No. 1, pp. 5-24.

Gladwell, M. (2010), *Outliers: The Story of Success*, Little, Brown and Company, Boston, MA.

Glastra, F.J. and Meerman, M. (2012), Developing Ethnic Talent in the Dutch National Tax Administration: A Case Study, *European Journal of Training and Development,* Vol. 36, No. 1, pp. 105-124.

Heinen, S.J. and O'Neill, C. (2004), Managing Talent to Maximize Performance, *Employment Relations Today,* Vol. 31, p. 2.

Heller, K.A., Monks, F.J., Subotnik, R.F. and Sternberg, R.J. (2000), *International Handbook of Giftedness and Talent*, Elsevier, Oxford.

Lewis, R.E. and Heckman, R.J. (2006), Talent Management: A Critical Review, *Human Resource Management Review,* Vol. 16, No. 2, pp. 139-54.

Longman Dictionary of Contemporary English (2006), Longman Dictionary of Contemporary English, Pearson ESL, London.

Michaels, E., Handfield-Jones, H. and Axelrod, B. (2001), *The War for Talent*, Harvard Business School Press, Boston, MA.

Oxford Reference English Dictionary, Indian Edition (2008).

Ozhegov, S.I. (ed.) (1984), *Slovar' russkogo yazyka* (Dictionary of the Russian Language), Russkii Yazyk, Moscow.

Philip, L. and Chauhan, C.P. (11th March 2011), *Maruti Revamps Talent Management Norms Over Attrition Fears*, ET Bureau.

Politikens (2000), *Politikens Nu Dansk med Etymologi L.-A.*, Politikens Vorlag, Copenhagen.

Ready, D.A., Conger, J.A. and Hill, L.A. (2010,. Are You a High Potential?. *Harvard Business Review,* Vol. 88, No. 6, pp. 78-84.

Romans, J. and Lardner, L. (2005), Integrated Talent Management at BD Japan, *Strategic Human Resource Review,* Vol. 4, No. 5, pp. 16-19.

Scheweyer, A. (2004), *Talent Management Systems: Best Practices in Technology Solutions for Recruitment, Retention and Workforce Planning*, Wiley, New York, NY.

Simonton, D.K. (1999), Talent and its Development: An Emergenic and Epigenetic Model, *Psychological Review,* Vol. 106, No. 3, pp. 435-457.

Singh, R., Ragins, B.R. and Tharenou, P. (2009), Who Gets a Mentor? A Longitudinal Assessment of the Rising Star Hypothesis, *Journal of Vocational Behaviour,* Vol. 74, No. 1, pp. 11-17.

Sloboda, J.A. (1985), *The Musical Mind*, Clarendon Press, Oxford.

Tansley, C. (2011), What do We Mean by the Term Talent in Talent Management? *Industrial and Commercial Training,* Vol. 43, No. 5, pp. 266-274.

Tansley, C., Harris, L., Stewart, J. and Turner, P. (2007), *Talent Management: Strategies, Policies and Practices,* Chartered Institute of Personnel and Development, London.

Tranckle, P. and Cushion, C.J. (2006), Rethinking Giftedness and

Talent, *Sport Quest,* Vol. 58, No. 2, pp. 265-82.

Whelan, E. and Carcary, M. (2011), Integrating Talent and Knowledge Management: Where are the Benefits? *Journal of Knowledge Management,* Vol. 15, No. 4, pp. 675-687.

9

An Insight into Gender Diversity

Chinmaya Kumar Podder

Diversity is generally defined as acknowledging, understanding, accepting, valuing and celebrating differences among people with respect to age, class, ethnicity, gender, physical and mental ability, sexual orientation, spiritual practice and public assistance.

It has also been defined as the variety of experiences and perspectives which arise from differences culture, religion, mental or physical abilities, heritage, age, gender, sexual orientation and other characteristics

Gender diversity means the proportion of males to females in the workplace. This can have an effect on how people interact and behave with one another in the workplace and would impact culture and social environment. Gender diversity discussions tend to focus on three main concerns:

1. The relationship between corporate profitability and gender diversity.
2. The problem of recruiting and retaining women professional where corporate culture can be inhospitable.
3. The number of women entering and graduating from science, engineering and mathematics programme etc.

Why is Gender Diversity so Important?

First let us examine how gender diversity positively impacts the bottom line in terms of profitability, return on equity (ROE) and total return to share holder (TRS). A study in 2001 by Rye Adler "Women in the executive suites correlate to high profits" published by Glass Ceiling Research Centre, found that 25 percent Fortune 500 firms with the best record of promoting women to high positions are between 18 to 69 percent more profitable. According to a 2004 study conducted by Catalysts, the bottom line connecting corporate performance and gender diversity examined 355 Fortune 500 companies from 5 industries—consumer discretionary, consumer staple, financial, industrial and IT/ telecommunication services. The study found that the companies with the highest representation of women show better financial performance than companies with lowest women representation. These findings hold for both financial measures analysis—ROE which is 35 percent higher and TRS which is 34 percent higher.

Furthermore, diversity can encourage a more balanced view of problem and increased richness in decision-making through consideration of different viewpoints and perspectives. Diversity has also been shown to strengthen the overall corporate culture, enhanced corporate reputation, act as a recruitment and retention tool, enhanced service levels, reduced turnover and lower absenteeism rate and improve company's global management capacity. Diversity creates a sense of worldliness which otherwise would not be possible.

No. of studies show that women have more social sensitivities and higher emotional intelligence level which enable them to deal with people with different temperament better and hence prove to be more successful as project managers than their male counterparts. Studies show that greater is the diversity of a team in an organisation, greater is the possibility of innovation and problem solving. Statistics also show that companies with women on the board are more successful than without.

Women leaders foster a better environment and bring a strong team orientation into the culture. There have also been studies to show women leaders are more stable and loyal to the organisation. They bring in greater stability and are less prone to attrition. An internal study in 2001 at IBM shows that women leaders scored better than the male counterparts in the following categories: customer insight, team leadership, team work, building organisation, capability, personal dedication and commitment and innovation. All of this adds up to economic value as the study at IBM shows having more women, profits the organisation.

Increased profitability and greater return to shareholder may be incentive for other companies to more effectively manage greater diversity and appoint more female representatives to their executive teams. However, to get there, the companies need to take certain steps:

Step 1: Encourage male and female co-workers to communicate with one another. With more women in the workforce men must recognise that women like to talk out the ideas and problem. If a woman comes to a male colleague to discuss a problem she probably just needs someone to listen and not someone to solve the problem. Likewise a woman should not take it personally when a male colleague openly vents his frustration of anger. Although the loss of control may not be appropriate in the workplace, anger is a common male reaction to stress universally. Gender differences are as common in a workplace as individual differences.

Step 2: Find a middle ground. Men and women differ in how they communicate, therefore a company can benefit by employees of both gender to recognise their differences and appreciate each other for the mixed strategies they can bring to the company. One example is the value of intuition of women which often play a key role in decision-making.

Step 3: Ensure that women are not left out of management opportunities because they have taken time out of their career to raise family.

Step 4: Discourage the "Good old boys club" mentality, one of the largest barriers of women in many companies. A woman can find it difficult to move upward in a company if her family values are at odds with that of male competing r the same position.

Step 5: Rate individual achievement within the company.

According to research conducted at Stanford Graduate School of Business, those companies which employ highest number of women are larger, growing more rapidly and have formal employment policies in place. The study shows that companies that place high value on individual achievement rather than how well an employee fits in with the company's culture or their peers have more women on the payrolls.

Step 6: Change company policies or organisation structure as needed. The key for successful gender diversity within a company is the willingness to make changes. The strategy becomes more essential when there is not a good representation of women in a company.

Step 7: Mentor others working for the company. Those who hold management and executive positions at a company can encourage other women and help to create a more gender diverse culture within the organisation by offering support, advice and direction.

Best Practices in Gender Diversity

Microsoft: At leadership levelm diversity is on their performance scorecard. At Microsoft offices in many countries, it is proven when there is a positive impact on business. They take diversity very seriously.

Procter & Gamble: The leadership team is accountable for career progression of women. At P&G, India there is leadership accountability of diversity at every level and at every function even in manufacturing and sales. The entire leadership team has diversity on its scorecard. The company tracks the success of high-potential women. If there is a big skew, the leadership intervenes. P&G has 30 percent women across level and half of its leadership team is women. Internal women's network is also a key enabler for driving gender diversity in the company.

Accenture: At Accenture, India gender diversity is part of CXO and leadership scorecard. Each of the leaders from top-down is assessed on gender diversity.

Crisil: The word diversity was not in the vocabulary of companies when it started 25 years back. Today, it is on the agenda of management and boards.

Anthelio: The leading independent provider of comprehensive health care information technology services and business process solution for hospitals and other health care providers received the NASSCOM award for excellence in gender inclusivity and diversity. NASSCOM has recognised Anthelio for its efforts in creating a culture in which women employees are encouraged to achieve their full potential and advance leadership positions. The company has proven that it believes in working with principles like gender equity at all levels of hierarchy.

Barclays: In Barclays, gender is a key strand of the diversity and inclusion program with a focus on employing more women. In 2008, 25 percent of the Bank's senior managers were women up from 20 percent in 2007. Two primary factors which enable women executives to reach higher echelons at Barclays are: (i) Environment that supports work life balance, and (ii) Robust mentor-mentee framework within the organisation.

IBM, India: IBM feels gender diversity is a compelling business imperative and hence they value women employees as a core component of their business strategy. To reiterate IBM's commitment to gender diversity they have setup Indian Women's Leadership Council which brings in required focus on gender diversity for the entire organisation. The programmes are driven to attract and retain and grow talent, to create a strong accountability, mechanism that ensures adherence to the gender diversity focus in India and South-Asia. IBM extends support to their women employees which is perhaps unparallel in the industry—from one of the best children care/dependent care services to a range of work life flexibility options.

Infosys: Women constitute 33 percent of the total work-force. Infosys Women Inclusivity Network (IWIN) promotes gender sensitive work environment. IWIN recognises the unique aspirations and needs of the women. It provides avenues for vocational, personal, and psychological counsel to enable professional and personal development.

Two years ago, Infosys started to evaluate the ratio of male to female eligible managers and the male bias in the ratio pushed them to investigate the causes and bring about changes in policy, such as including one women representative in promotion and hiring. The company found that the move increased the number of eligible female managers. In the past three months, the company introduced two new policies, one of which would groom first time female managers on job-related competencies and would educate them on behavioural differences from their male counterparts. The second was aimed at providing formal mentoring and counselling. They have found dramatic increase in the number of women eligible for management roles since these programmes were introduced.

WIPRO: Women constitute 30 percent of the total talent pool at Wipro. Wipro has extensive programmes that promote growth of women in the organization such as "Women in leadership", mentoring for success and the women of Wipro speaker series. Wipro has sustainability council formed with the objective of creating a dynamic and powerful socio-business network, which fosters a sensitive and equal opportunity environment, which allows every individual to realise their fullest potential.

TCS: TCS is an equal opportunity employer and has been involved in supporting diversity in workplace for many years now. In order to strengthen and reaffirm the commitment to diversity, "Diversity and Women Network (DAWN)" was launched three years ago. Its intent is to sharpen focus and heighten sensitivity on the diversity mandate across the various location and business units and it brings all activities under one banner.

TCS has implemented several initiatives to create

increased awareness and shift of mindset towards gender inclusion. Some of the initiatives include a stay-connected and reorientation programme for associates once they proceed and return from a long leave, day-care tie-ups, work-place parents' group and discussion forums.

To empower talented women and help them realise their potential, an executive education programme was launched this year. The aim is to help them become more self-aware, develop a personal brand and get a better insight into the larger organizational context. This initiative attempts to help TCS build a more sustainable leadership pipeline and retain and engage with extraordinary women talent. In TCS, 30 percent of the talent pool is women, and at senior management level it is about 11 percent.

India's Ranking in Gender Diversity amongst Top Asian Countries

India is worst among top six Asian economies when it comes to the representation of women in the workforce at junior and middle level positions, according to the gender diversity benchmark for Asia 2011 report. It performs only slightly better than Japan at senior level positions. The report surveyed women at different levels across 21 countries–in China, Hong Kong, India, Japan, Malaysia and Singapore. Participants included a mix of consulting, financial services, technology and fast moving consumer goods (FMCG companies) including Ernst & Young, Bank of America, Merrill Lynch, Cisco Systems and Coca-Cola. The study underlines gender bias in India, where social attitude still privilege the male as the dominant educated earning member of the family, with the female being the home-maker.

China has the highest percentage of women representation in the total workforce (49.7 percent) followed by Malaysia (47.35 percent), Hong Kong (45.34 percent), Singapore (43.29 percent). The least percentage of women is employed in India (24.43 percent) with Japan (33.67 percent), the second lowest according to the study.

Conclusion

The business case for gender diversity asserts that organisations that support and promote women will benefit for a number of reasons specifically they will access a large part of the available talent pool as well as employ individuals who reflect a substantial part of the consumer base. The business mantra is, "every man contains a woman inside to do any business, every woman should contain a man inside to sustain the operation". If the employers in India want to make it easier for young women in the workforce, they need to create policies—be it maternity, flexibility or mentoring specific age group and gender.

10

Employer Branding: Essentials and Strategies

Chinmaya Kumar Podder

Introduction

A brand can be associated with a product or service or a person or could even be a company. For example, Google is a known brand but if you are looking for a job, Google is an employer brand.

Employment branding is a targeted long-term strategy to manage the awareness and perception of employees and related stakeholders with regard to a particular firm. The strategy can be turned to drive recruitment, retention and productivity of management. It happens when organizations consistently put efforts for building an image that surrounds management and business practices which makes the organization attractive—a great place to work. The immediate result of successful branding is that your organization's exposure and reputation increases, creating consensus among your employees and high potential applicants.

Essential Elements of Employment Branding

Employment branding is a targeted-coordinated strategy and must contain following eight essential elements.

1. A Culture of Sharing and Continuous Improvement: No employment brand effort can succeed in an organisation that is afraid to expose best management practices. Unless your firm wants to be left behind, becoming more and more obscure each year, it is essential that senior management recognises and encourages employment branding and the sharing of best practices. Therefore, the foundation element of a good employment brand is senior management team that encourages, measures and rewards the development and sharing of best practices.

2. A Balance between Good Management and High Productivity: Having unique benefits and good community work, both have some impact on a firm's external image. However, the primary foundation of any employment brand is first and foremost, the firm's management practices that go overboard in an effort to look good. This look good effort might result in managers becoming overtly soft or losing the focus on the importance of maintaining and increasing the productivity of the workforce. Since the basis for any HR effort should be to increase workforce productivity, any image building effort must balance look good and increasing productivity.

3. Getting Public Recognition: There is no doubt that the increased interest in employment branding during the past decade has been a direct result of the increased number of organisations that create lists of great places to work. While it is true that many of these lists are heavily slanted against the benefit of exposure that occurs as a result of being listed, this exposure increases the credibility of your firm and reinforces the mindset amongst target audience that your organisation is a good place to work.

4. Employees Proactively Telling Stories: One of the prime attributes of a great employment brand is that employees go out of their way to tell stories about the firm's management, business practices and impact on their life. While almost any employee will respond to a question about the firm, employees at well branded firms volunteer their stories to strangers both inside and outside their workplace. Having created such an environment enables viral marketing, where the employees spread the word about great management practices to their friends, co-workers and even the strangers on the air plane; at places like professional meetings and social settings. In well branded firms, even the employees' families know of and help spread stories.

5. Getting Talked About: The number of agencies that make up the business press has grown so large and become so segmented and influential that being talked in specific publications has been an essential element in building a strong employment brand. Having others talked about you and cite your great management practices has more impact than any employment advertisement that you could place. Getting talked about requires two basic components: first, managers must speak and write about their management practices in highly visible ways, and second, component of getting talked about focuses on getting written up in the business press.

6. Becoming a Benchmark Firm: The best managed firms are also known as benchmark firms. These are the firms that have best practices that everyone wants to learn about and emulate. A good brand needs management to take part in major benchmarking studies and to try for a conscious effort to respond to those who highlight your best practices.

7. Increasing Candidates Awareness of Best Practices: There are many companies that are well known because of their product brand but have not developed awareness for their management practices. A great management brand does not just increases the potential applicants' awareness of the firm, rather it goes one step further and informs potential applicants about management practices that make an organisation, a great place to work. The basic foundation of the branding step is to craft messages to your target audience of potential applicants so that they apply for your job specifically for your management and business practices.

8. Branding Assessment Metrics: Employment brand must continually change and improve the key to that continuous improvement is the issue of brand assessment measures or metrics. Any branding campaign should begin with side by side comparison numbers that can be used to judge the relative success and improvement of the effort. Branding metrics should be the part of assessment metrics for all major business functions and their managers.

Six Steps to an Employer Branding Strategy

Having a clearly defined strategy is the most important factor in achieving employer branding objectives. That is the takeaway from Employer Brand Institutes, 'Global Research Study' of more than 2,000 companies.

The take away from the research is that you need to focus on six key areas to develop an employer brand strategy that will assist you in achieving your programme objectives.

1. Determine How Employer Branding is Viewed Inside Your Company: You should define what your employer branding means to your company. Your employer brand is the image of your organisation as a great place to work in the mind of current employees and key stakeholders in the external market. Employer branding is therefore concerned with the attraction engagement and retention initiative target at enhancing your company's employer brand. If you take a narrow focus on employer branding, it is likely to end up as a departmental project that is not aligned with the overall business strategy. For example, if you believe employer branding is only about recruitment, it is likely your organisation have already closed up shop of employer branding as a result of economic meltdown while your competitors may be investing on the same as a long-term strategy to attract and retain talent.

2. Define Brand Objective and Project Scope: Defining your objectives up front will save you time and money in the long-run and keep your programme on time and budget. Companies have different lifecycle stages and therefore will have different objectives at different stages.

3. The Relationship between HR, Marketing and Communication: Ownership of the strategy is often a grey area that should be clearly defined. Hence, all key stakeholders achieve consensus and are united in the objectives to obtain both budget and buy–in human resources often HR has to drive employer branding through internal education and awareness building.

4. Discovering Your Employer Brand: The key to developing your brand strategy is to arrive at a comprehensive understanding of the organisation's culture, work experience, key talent drivers, external perceptions, leadership vision, and management practices. Operating from this position of intelligence supports the construct of a message platform that is authentic, compelling, differentiated, and that would be internally accepted and received in the outside market, and continuously delivering upon by the organisation.

5. CEO and Senior Management: It pays to have conversation about 100 brands with CEO and senior management in the early stages of developing your strategy. Areas for discussions could include:

- How well an employer brand supports our business strategy—growth, mergers and acquisitions (M&A), and consolidation?
- What kind of culture do we have across geographical and divisional boundaries?
- What behaviours are felt to be most characteristic of the organisation?
- What is the most useful way of segmenting employee population?
- How consistent is the message we are communicating internally and externally about our organisation, 'as a great place to work'?
- What are the most effective channels of communication?
- What are the critical positions and what we are currently doing to attract, engage and retain them?

6. Communication Planning: There is a plethora of offline and online channels available to communicate your employees' value proposition to your target audience, including web, print, social network, events, and public relations. The key is to test and trial the channels and arrive at a communication strategy for minimum investment.

Companies like Standard Chartered Bank and Philips ensure that a consistent brand is communicated globally through recruitment and communication with change for local nuances, such as language. This does not only ensures brand positioning but also saves design costs and increases the campaign spend in the market.

In the absence of a clearly defined strategy, your employer brand is likely to fall flat. Taking a strategic approach at your employer brand programme is likely to result in senior management's engagement and allocation of resources required to effectively build competitive advantage. Google, PwC, Mckinsey & Co. have consistently achieved this overtime and are regularly ranked high as best places to work.

Employer Branding in India: A Survey Report

In a survey conducted by TimesJob.com, it was revealed that employer branding is not very prevalent in Indian industry. However, they do believe that companies with strong employer brands can potentially reduce the cost of employee acquisition, improve employee retention and employee relation. The latest research report throws light on the fact—overall 24 percent say that they have a clear employer branding strategy; more than 40 percent claim, yes they have a strategy but it could be developed further and another 20 percent say that they do not have one but they are working on it which could be interpreted as such a strategy still not on their priority agenda; another 40 percent state the lack of senior management engagement as a challenge which is again symptomatic of the lack of vision on the organisation's part.

Guidelines for Building an Employer Brand in India

1. Every employer brand is an investment that should demonstrate a return comparable to other form of business investment.
2. Offer a strong value proposition to talent in India.
3. Employer branding is as much about retention and

engagement as much as it is about recruitment. Retain the core of brand and contextualise development.

4. Keep the local content in mind. Recognise, accept and adapt to the local culture.
5. The employer brand should include the sensitivity aspect of employees' in foreign countries.
6. The advertisement of the employer and employee brand should be synergetic and mutually rewarding.

Conclusion

Employer branding and actions required to build and manage an employer's brand, adds value to one's organization through HR. Very often, HR seems to impact on the bottom line of the firm by containing cost containment initiatives. Such initiatives do not enhance the quality or productivity. Employment branding on the other hand, can enhance the quality of employees and inspire them to be very productive. Thus, employment branding can address many of the corporate issues today. Ignoring it may be a sure way to ensure a spot in the corporate graveyard. The case for taking employer branding seriously is compelling. In an economic environment where business is tough, there is a pressure to cut costs and increase productivity. This makes the need to get the right people for right job more crucial. An attractive employer can create for employees' an illusion that their choices are limited outside of the organisation, constantly maintaining an image of being the most desirable employer and giving the right reasons or incentives for their top performers to stay.

References

Employer Branding in India: A Survey Report, *timesjob.com*, dated 12th March 2012.

Michington, B. and Estic, R. (2012), 6 Steps to an Employer Brand Strategy, *ere.net,* dated 12th March 2012.

11

Employer Branding: A Human Resources Strategy

Mukesh Kumar Biswas

Introduction

Branding in HR book? Is it possible? Surprisingly, it is and is gradually making an entry into the HR syllabus. The interest for science of branding in HR has captured the likes of academics and students as they are undertaking more and more researches in related topics viz. corporate branding, HR branding, etc. But it is the employer branding that has established the concept of branding for human resource field and is being considered to be an important concept among all other HR topics.

How come the HR professionals and academicians are adopting the concept of branding, which is predominantly in custody of marketing function? A look into the current economy and employment scenario will reveal the truth. The business environment has become very dynamic and very competitive across the globe. Apart from few organizations that are in sectors like mining and energy to some extent, all other industries have to be on their toe everyday for their existence. The employment scenario is no more the same what it used to be a decade ago and has completely changed for most of the organizations; even the story for public sector is not different. A go-through of the many journal and periodical publications will reveal many factors that are affecting the employment scenario, viz. globalization, pressure for speed and innovation, widespread privatization, mergers and acquisitions, technology advancement, organization restructuring, and war for acquisition of talents.

A decade ago itself, Whymark and Ellis predicted that very few occupations will be able to offer "permanent jobs" or "jobs for life" and the number of safe fields of employment will gradually diminish. A new trend has set in the employment market. Now, talents are being sought after by organizations rather than talents looking for job in organizations. Further, the employees are also turning out to be portfolio workers [1] by nature. Thus, we see that the current economy has forced the researchers and HR practitioners to think beyond the regular HR topics. The economy now is quite different than what it used to be a couple of decades ago.

Further, one may argue that the population is growing; education has become better; lot of academic institutions have bloomed up; cost of living index is on a positive trend; and workforce in the employment market vis-à-vis unemployment is also growing—then how come the organizations are finding it difficult to get employees.

It is true that the workforce in the employment market is huge but what organizations need to have competitive advantage is a skilled workforce and talents. The irony is that talents are a rare species–shall be discussed later in this chapter. A talented human resource base has now taken the topmost place among all other factors for competitive advantage in any economic environment. As Peter Drucker [2] said, that businesses have traditionally been built on two dimensions: economic and human; the success of any organization now depends on how strong is its talent base. Historically, corporate leaders have looked to other functions, such as product development, marketing and sales, to drive corporate success. But today more and more eyes are looking towards HR as the call for need to identify talents from the employment market and find methods to attract and retain them in the organization for a longer period. This has made HR professionals to look into other fields and branding the HR functions came out to be one of the best possible ways to address the issue.

One can debate. You are a HR professional. Your job is to recruit people, manage people, train and develop people, and build and manage policies for the benefit of the people and the organization. So what does branding have to do with you and your profession? For this, first one should understand what is branding.

Branding

From a very early age, we are taught to create an image which will create a positive impact on others.

The very purpose of branding, as often made clear by marketing researchers, is to spread the advantage of a product over its competitors among the customers in a form of chain reaction similar to that of nuclear chain reaction [3], which we have studied in Science syllabi during middle school. It is said that a satisfied customer tells ten people about the experience while a satisfied employee tells hundred.

Branding is defined as "the process of building a favourable image for a product or company that differentiates it, in the minds of prospects and end users, from other competitors". Branding creates a positive image of anything be it a product or an organization or a corporate or even a human being in the minds of the people, thus drawing them towards it. It is an ongoing process of communication to multiple stakeholders. Hollensen (2007) gave four basic universal purposes of the branding process:

1. To distinguish an organization's offering and differentiate one particular product from its competitors.
2. To create identification and brand awareness.
3. To guarantee a certain level of quality and satisfaction.
4. To help with promotion of product or services.

If we would like to define branding in one line, it will be: Branding is the image or face of a subject.

HR branding has a similar intention like the normal branding. However, employer branding encompasses all other brandings of HR functions.

Employer Branding

You are going to have an employer brand, whether you know it or not. And you have two choices: you can intentionally create, shape, develop and track this brand or you can let it happen by accident. *–Kim Spivey*

Ambler and Barrow, for the first time, discussed the topic "Employer Branding" in their article in the journal of brand management in 1996. Since then, it has become a word-of-mouth in the corporate world and a lexicon in HR publications. It is recognised as one phenomenon or one strategy that can help an organization to face the challenge of talent crisis and outperform its competitors in securing an exceptional workforce.

Talent Challenges and Employer Branding

The demand for "top" talent is outpacing the available supply, thus creating what Clarke refers to as a "critical talent and skill shortages in virtually all industries requiring specialized core competencies within the workforce". It is important to note that "top" in this definition does not refer to the place in the organization chart or structure, rather it is indicative of the best employee, the top performer for each position in the organization. The talent scarcity is due to the growing number of retirees, emergence of new jobs, competitive business environment, open market, and competing job offers. In addition, talents are increasingly mobile, have highly transferable skills, and are well informed. Highly talented graduates can always find work, even in an economic slowdown.

This uncertainty about talents has forced organizations to review their employee relation strategies in terms of attraction, motivation, and retention of talents that are actually the prime factors to be successful. (Zivnuska, Ketchen, and Snow, 2001) Actually, it won't be wrong if the current economy is marked predominantly by the war of talent from strategic point of view. Talent attraction and retention has, therefore, become a hard hitting issue for many organizations and they are forced to consider their options like never before. In fact, organizations started recognising the importance to expand the recruitment areas beyond domestic borders to meet their talent demand.

This deficit seems to be contrary to the reported higher levels of unemployment being experienced in many countries, yet it is not the numbers of workers that is in deficit, rather, it is a lack of skills. In 2002, Johnson rightly said, "the skill shortage is so critical now-a-days that it will be those organizations that can successfully position themselves as a 'magnet' for talent will gain advantage". How to develop the talent magnet is when the strategy of employer branding is being thought of.

"If you don't engage me, somebody else will"–the current belief

Given the economy and the fact that there is an acute shortage of talent, the new age employee is emboldened to actually make a choice to move on to better suited pastures, one that takes the extra step of engaging employees through some means of unique differentiation.

Today globally and locally, organizations as diverse as Google, Microsoft, TATA Group, NTPC, Deloitte, Ranbaxy and Wipro are using employer branding as a tool to acquire, retain and engage talents. Even the not-for-profit organizations such as the Red Cross and governmental organizations like the Indian Air Force have been making use of employer branding for some time. In fact, according to Harding, way back in 2003, many organizations in practice have been making use of the idea knowingly or unknowingly. A lot of researches are being carried out in this field as over the last 5 years.

By the year 2010, Edwards argued that the interest for employer branding has grown so tremendously that it has become an important strategic tool for HR practitioners to win the talent war. CIPD (2007) report has attributed four main reasons to the rise of employer branding and its importance for HR: (a) the power of brand, (b) the increasing focus of employee engagement, (c) the prevailing of labour market at the time and the war for talent, and (d) HR's ongoing search for credibility. The evident is from the numerous publications on the topic in the business and popular press and is quite obvious.

Another interesting development in this field is the Employer Brand Awards started by the Employer Branding Institute in 2008. The awards have become very competitive across Europe, in some areas of the US, and in parts of the Asia-Pacific region, including Singapore, Malaysia and India. The attention of these awards in India has been in focus recently, owing to the growth and opportunity in employment that the country has been experiencing.

Since economic liberalization in 1990s, more and more foreign companies and MNCs started investing in India due to high business opportunities and availability of cheap and skilled workforce. It did not take much time to realise that the employment market is comparatively much more mobile and unstable in India and thus very difficult to attract and retain employees. The companies therefore started taking keen interest to differentiate themselves both in their products and organisation structure and policies from their competitors to attract people to the company.

As Jorgensen (2005) puts up, that employer branding is a notion of 'employer of choice'. Researchers like Lenaghan, Eisner, Mackes and many more has provided evidences that one such strategy employed by Western organizations facing direct competition for high-quality employees has been to present themselves as an 'Employer of Choice' in their respective industry. Organizations these days want to be the best choice for talents entering the employment market.

What is Employer Branding?

According to Ambler and Barrow, employer branding can be defined in terms of 'benefits' such as a package of economic (e.g. reward and remuneration), functional (e.g.

training, skills and other job related activities for development), and psychological (e.g. identity, recognition, and belonging) benefits provided by employment, and identified with the employing organization. Sullivan defined the term as "a targeted, long-term strategy to manage the awareness and perceptions of employees, potential employees, and related stakeholders with regards to a particular firm".

Employer branding is a concept which can be applied to the recruitment process in the same way as marketing process used in the management of customers. Yet, employer branding is not just a marketing exercise–it is the beginning of an employment relationship.

A simple way to understand the concept can be through marketing language i.e. can be interpreted in a similar way as product branding. In employer branding, the 'product' is the 'employment experience' of an employer, and the 'markets' are 'prospective and existing employees' of an organization across a range of skill sets and demographic features. Thus, employment experience is the underlying foundation for employer branding. Edwards (2010) argues that values and influences are created when organizations clarify and carefully manage their 'employment experience'.

This employment experience is referred as 'employment value proposition (EVP)'. This value proposition consists of the whole cluster of benefits the organization promises to its employees, as discussed by Ambler and Barrow: (a) economic (e.g. reward and remuneration), (b) functional (e.g. training, skills and other job related activities for development), and (c) psychological (e.g. identity, recognition, and belonging). A study by Conference Board shows that only 20 percent increase in salaries are required to attract new employees for an organization with attractive EVP, juxtaposed to 34 percent increase in the same with unattractive EVP.

Employment Value Proposition (EVP)

In 1999, the Corporate Leadership Council released a

report in which they stressed upon the employment offer i.e. a strong employment value proposition (EVP). Beyond the opportunity to work for a company with a leading product or company brand, these offers are composed of selected levels of compensation and benefits, work environment, work/life balance and company culture. The more the ability of a company to deliver on its employees the more enhanced will be the employer brand image of the company.

In essence, employer branding is the application of marketing, communications and branding concepts to promises of an employment experience that make an organization distinctive and appealing to new and existing employees, and ensuring that employees identify and engage with the organization, its corporate brand, mission, values and beliefs and thrive with it. Having a strong employer brand is like the organization's charismatic personality. Who you are draws others to you. If we consider employees as customers and 'employment experience' as the 'product' being offered for their consideration and purchase—the 'customer satisfaction' would then reflect the 'strength' of the employer branding. Similar to the product branding, which creates a lasting image in the mind of consumers about the organization's products for quality and service, Employer branding creates an 'image' of the employer among employees for its employment. Organizations with higher involvement in employer branding are generally well managed organizations where employees are motivated, continually learning and growing. Strong employer brand has a magnetic effect when it comes to attracting and retaining good people.

In short, employer branding is defined as the sum of a company's efforts to communicate to existing and prospective employees what makes it a desirable place to work and the active management of a company's image as seen through the eyes of its associates and potential hires.

In 2009, Rosethorn defined the employer branding as an art: "...the two-way deal between an organization and its people—the reason they choose to join and the reasons they choose—and are permitted—to stay. The art of employer branding is to articulate this deal in a way that is distinctive, compelling and relevant to the individual, and to ensure that it is delivered throughout the lifecycle of the employee within organizations."

Simon Barrow described four elements that work together to define an employer brand.

1. The employment package includes those things that often "close the deal" for the prospective employee, such as financial compensation, work/life balance, the employee's role in organization and professional development.
2. Culture and environment includes items such as the physical working environment, the size of the organization, and the organization's approach to work. Brand image and reputation equals integrity. Employer branding without integrity is evident when job seekers are hired only to discover a ruse; the organization stated things that were not true. The consequence of a lack of integrity is the employee does not stay with the organization long, contributing to the organization's turnover costs. To attract people to something you cannot deliver, is a waste of your time and money.
3. Management performance is a vital part in the employer branding process. Senior management must be committed and involved in recruitment or the Employer branding process will be a failure.

It is pertinent to mention now that there is little consensus on the conceptualization of the term 'employer branding' among the practitioners. A solid single model is yet to be developed. This indicates how dynamic the concept of employer branding is. The field is yet to develop fully and hence there is much more scope for the researchers.

Employer Brand Building Process

Developing an image as an employer is part of employer

branding. Turning that image into a working relationship between an organization and its potential recruits is a process. There are many publications on employer branding process by practitioners and researchers alike. As already mentioned, there is no universal model available for employer branding. However, in this section let us notice the various but prominent methods of employer brand building process.

Typical employer branding objectives could be:

1. To enhance the company's appeal to attract talent.
2. To create alignment of employees to org mission and objectives.
3. To convey the role and importance of the organizational mission.
4. To position the company's brand amongst employees and improve its brand equity.
5. To benchmark the organization for best practices.

Melin describes employer branding in two levels. Level one is creating the employer brand identity, which is the actual employment offer or job offer designed and provided by the organization. This is the wanted projected version of the employer brand that the organization sends out to the labour market. This employer brand identity created with the intention of being the most compelling employment offer under the "employer of choice" framework. Level two is creating the employer brand image, which is based on the perception of employees towards the employer brand identity that is projected to the labour market by the organization. Internal employer brand image is the perceived employer brand identity by the organization's own employees and the external employer brand image being the perceived employer brand identity by people in general and prospective employees in specific.

Backhaus and Tikoo outlined employer branding process into three steps. First, developing a concept of the particular value, an organization offers to prospective and current employees. An organization has to do a thorough research in this step as it involves developing propositions that becomes the central message conveyed by EB. Second, marketing externally these determined value propositions to the targeted applicant population. Third, carrying the brand promises to the recruitee and incorporating it as part of the organizational culture.

Ahmed, Rafiq and Norizan showed that employer branding needs a more integrated internal mix consisting of three groups: (a) top management group—support, empowerment, vision and leadership, strategic and conducive environment, (b) business processing group—staffing, operational or process changes, and incentive systems, and (c) cross-functional group—HR, internal communication, corporate communication and marketing.

Jorgensen defines the dimension of employer branding within the "employer of choice" framework of the characteristics of good jobs: (a) quality and balance, (b) procedures, (c) compensation, (d) people, (e) work, and (f) opportunity. The dimension "quality and balance" refers to providing a quality workplace for all staff. The dimension of "procedures" looks at the degree of empowerment the organization provides to its subunits to act by providing flexible resource and supportive collaborative practice. "Compensation" measures whether individual effort and group success are valued, recognized and rewarded. The dimension of "people" looks at the degree of individual participation that is enabled by inclusive leadership and targeted training. "Work" refers to the facilitation of multi-skilled individuals in cross-functional teams across a networked community and finally the dimension of "opportunity" measures whether the workforce is able to grow through tailored learning and adoption of multi-aged employment practices.

C. Mahalingam (senior V.P. and chief people officer with Symphony Services Corporation) provides two interesting approaches to employer branding. The first one is the "outside-in" approach where a company focus on creating visibility for it in the target talent markets through a multi-faceted approach including well-designed websites with content on the company culture, compensation practices, and career opportunities and why it is a great place to work. The other one is the 'inside-out' approach whereby a company create powerful branding internally through employee experience and turn its employees into brand advocates. The approach is in synonymous with the universal truth that HR professionals interact with two kind of customers.

Brett Minchington, Chairman/CEO of Employer Brand International has developed a roadmap that helps companies to develop their employer brand. The roadmap is divided in 4 phases: concept, design, integration and evaluation.

Concept Phase: There are four steps that start with first defining the employer brand project scope, identifying the stakeholders involved, conducting research internally and externally and assessing the results by determining the most optimal segment. HR is mainly responsible for this phase, in the first step employees are also involved and in the assessment (third) step, other functions such as marketing, communications. The senior management is also involved to a certain extent.

Design Phase: Employer brand identity and image is defined and reviews are given from the senior management.

Integration Phase: HR aligns the employer brand management system with the people management policies procedures and practices, and the employer brand communication plan is created.

Evaluation Phase: The HR functions define the metrics and measure the return on investment and review results with senior management.

The measures for employer branding is still at its nascent stage. The need for a solid measuring tool is common across all those whoever is associated with employer branding activities. It is difficult to measure the return-of-investment (ROI) tangibly in a very short period. The most common suggestions of many practitioners and researchers in published articles can be aggregated as: (a) conducting a campus survey in identified campuses among passing out batch with a list of 3 to 5 companies in respective sector, (b) conducting employee survey, e.g. employee satisfaction survey, etc. and (c) measuring factors such as incoming employees' skills, knowledge and ability, and annual turnover as well as individual level productivity, or aggregate level productivity.

Consequences of Employer Branding

According to Sullivan, a successful employer branding strategy does the following:

1. It develops a common theme so that current workers tell friends and contacts a similar story about what it is like to be an employee of the firm.
2. It builds and reinforces the public's image of the firm's culture, work practices, management style and growth opportunities.
3. It coordinates the employment brand with the company's brand and its different product brands.
4. It continually monitor the firm's employment image both inside and outside the firm to ensure the brand image remains strong.
5. It energises the best potential candidates to apply for jobs at the firm.

When properly planned and executed an employer branding initiative can generate lively dialogue between an employer and its employees build a rationale for a 'mutual working arrangement' and establish compelling reasons to commit to the arrangement.

'Employer brand power' adds value to the recruitment process and real money to organizations. It gets you noticed and creates an 'employer of choice'. As the number of possible choices graduates can make is becoming even greater in the marketplace and as globalization impacts increasingly, employer branding strategies prove critical. Employer brands act as a psychological trigger in candidate's heads. These are very powerful triggers in the job market and can play a key role in candidate's job choice.

Employer Brands, Product Brands and Corporate Brands: What are the Differences?

Although product brands, corporate brands and employer brands seem to be analogous to each other, there are fundamental differences: this is an issue that has concerned researchers for more than a decade. (King, 1991; Balmer, 1995; De Chernatony, 1999) Table 11.1 illustrates the key differences between employer brands and product brands.

Table 11.1: A Comparison between Product Brands and Employer Brands

	Product Brand	Employer Brand
Focus of attention on	The product	The company
Management responsibility	Middle management/ brand manager	Top level managers
Functional responsibility	Marketing	Whole company, mainly HR
Stakeholder focus	Customers/consumers	Multiple stakeholders
Communicated by	Marketing communications	Multiple communications
Time horizon	Short (product life)	Long (company life)
Importance to organization	Tactical for function	Strategic for organization

Source: employerbrand.com

The branding of products has been a very important strategy of a company and essentially a very important job of marketing department. The product branding enables the company to keep customers loyal and also attract new customers to the product, which is necessary to keep the business going. A few years ago, when Nokia opened one of its plants in India, it was highly a topic of conversation among people. People were happy to get a company which produces the highly purchased mobile. The product thus made the opening of the company a successful venture. It would not have possible, if Nokia sets were not so in demand. Similarly, the employer brand is the branding of an employer.

The greater the brand of the employer, the more the people would like to associate with the employer. People would proudly say that they work for TATA or GE. The company does not face any difficulty in attracting the best talent from the employment market. In addition, the employees of the company become loyal to the company and do not leave it unless the circumstances are against. Talented employees always produce products which are different and fulfil the customers' requirements, thus keeping the brand of the product. So, product brand and employer brand go hand in hand.

Tuzuner and Yuksel (2009) has explored two key differences that distinguish employer brand development over the firm's product brand and corporate brand (Table 11.2): (a) the employer brand is employment specific, characterizing the firm's identity as an employer, and (b) it is directed at both internal and external audiences whereas product and corporate branding efforts are primarily directed to external audience. The experience of employer brand by employees of a firm is substantively different than that experienced by consumers for product or corporate brands.

Brand Equity and Job Choice

Brand equity is defined as the "marketing effects or outcome that accrues to a product with its brand name compared with those that would accrue if the same product did not have the brand name."

As the definition indicates, the brand name leads to differential effects or outcomes. The outcomes that have been examined pertained to consumers (i.e. awareness, consideration set, choice, and willingness to pay a higher price). Given that the outcomes studied dealt with consumer decision making, by extension, job decision making may be another possible outcome influenced by brand equity. Research has found that product information influenced job seekers perception of the company in terms of risk-taking and rules-orientation.

Table 11.2: A Comparison between Corporate Brands and Employer Brands

	Corporate Brand	Employer Brand
Focus of attention on	The corporate	The company
Management responsibility	Chief executive	Top level managers
Functional responsibility	Most/all departments	Whole company, mainly HR
Stakeholder focus	Multiple stakeholders	Multiple stakeholders
Communicated by	Total corporate communications	Multiple communications
Time horizon	Medium to long	Long (company life)
Importance to organization		Strategic for organization

Source: employerbrand.com

Why would we expect brand equity to influence people's job choice decisions? Consumer decisions and employment decisions may be similar. The consumer in choosing a product must be aware of the product, form a consideration set, and make the final choice from the consideration set. Research has shown that brand equity influences all three steps in the consumer decision making process. Similarly, qualified candidates in the job market must be aware of the company, consider the company a good place to work, and choose from a set of companies they consider appropriate. Given the similar decision steps, brand equity may influence job choice decisions because applicants will be more aware of the company, have a favourable disposition toward the product (which may transfer to the company) and subsequently influence their job choice.

In addition to similar steps in decision-making, the process underlying the effects of brand equity on consumer choice may also apply in a job choice situation. When applicants decide on which job offer to accept, they require information to make that choice. They may use their memory to retrieve the desired information. Research suggests that applicants rarely have full information about the organization's working conditions. Consequently, they will use other cues to infer missing information. One cue that is readily available in memory is the brand name. That person may have a positive attitude toward the brand and/or have emotional ties to the brand. Given the positive effect, this may lead to the inferences about the company that are positive in nature. These self-generated inferences may weigh heavily in their job choice decision.

Employer Brand: HR or Marketing

The debate of whether employer branding should be a part of marketing or HR department of a firm. Many academicians from both marketing and HR disciplines supported the view that interaction between the two disciplines occurs throughout the empioyer branding process. Many a practitioner feels that employer branding is not a HR function, in fact all functions play a role. Edwards summarised the concept in one go, that is employer branding is an activity where principles of marketing in particular the "science of branding", are applied to HR activities in relation to current and potential employees. Employer branding activities involves lot more than just creating a pretty website and setting of values. It should underpin everything that a company does, from the way it attracts and hires people, to the way they exit the business. Thus, HR professionals seem to have more said on employer branding activities.

Although the previous discussion clearly shows that employer branding is a part of human resource department; yet most HR departments are struggling with the challenges of understanding, measuring and then positioning their employer brands. What HR needs to understand is that employer branding is an opportunity to provide value to an organization at the strategic level.

Conclusion

As in marketing, brands seek to be chosen by customers. So the branding is an activity that is aimed at increasing the probability of being chosen by customers. The same lies with the concept of employer branding. In order to reach this goal, an employer must understand what its employees seek for. The human resource department has to advertise its activities and create a brand image in a way identical to the marketing of a product. For branding the HR is to perceive and acknowledge the needs of its employees. The changes in the market scenario bring about changes in the employee perceptions. It is the task of the HR to recognize the needs and formulate the policies of the company well before in advance.

The HR is to conduct the surveys of employees to realize the kind of image they have regarding the human resource department. A highly satisfied work force creates the best brand image for the HR. For HR branding, the HR is to identify the customer needs and perceptions regarding the functioning of the human resources and work for a better relationship. If there are differences in the employee and customer perceptions the HR is to take measures to nullify or minimize them to avoid the loss of business.

Definitions of Key Terms

Brand: A name, term, sign, symbol or design, or combination of them which is intended to identify the goods and services of one seller or group of sellers and to differentiate them from those of competitors.

Branding: Branding was originally used to differentiate tangible products, but over the years it has been applied to differentiating people, places and firms.

Employer Image: The naturally evolved way how an

employer is commonly perceived within a labour market.

Employer Brand: The employer brand establishes the identity of the firm as an employer. It encompasses the firm's value system, policies and behaviours toward the objectives of attracting, motivating, and retaining the firm's current and potential employees.

Employer Branding: A targeted, long-term strategy to manager the awareness and perceptions of employees, potential employees, and related stakeholders with regards to a particular firm.

Employer Value Proposition (EVP): An Employer's associations and offerings to its current and potential employees that differentiate it from recruitment competitors.

End Notes

1. According to Handy (1994), a portfolio worker gathers experience from projects in organizations and effectively defines their own career path as they progress from organization to organization, relying on much more on networking skills than being an "organization man".
2. Peter Drucker is one of the best-known and most widely influential thinkers and writers on the subject of management theory and practice.
3. Nuclear Chain Reaction occurs when one nuclear reaction causes an average of one or more nuclear reactions, thus leading to a self-propagating series of these reactions.

References

Ahmed, P.K., Rafiq, M. and Norizan, M.S. (2003), Internal Marketing and the Mediating Role of Organizational Competencies, *European Journal of Marketing, 37*(*9*), 1177-1186.

Ambler, T. and Barrow, S. (1996), The Employer Brand, *Journal of Brand Management, 4*, 185-206.

Backhaus, K. and Tikoo, S. (2004), Conceptualizing and Researching Employer Branding, *Career Development International, 9*, 501-517.

Balmer, J.M.T. and Gray, E.R. (2003), Corporate Brands: What Are They? What of Them? *European Journal of Marketing, 37*(*7/8*),

972-997.

Clarke, K. (2001), What Businesses are Doing to Attract and Retain Employees-Becoming an Employer of Choice, *Employee Benefits Journal*. 26(1), 21-24.

Chartered Institute of Personnel and Development (2007), *Employer Branding: The Latest Fad or the Future for HR?*

Corporate Leadership Council (1999), The Employer Brand: Building Competitive Advantage in the Labour Market, Corporate Leadership Council: Washington, D.C.

Edwards, M.R. (2010), An Integrative Review of Employer Branding and OB theory, *Personnel Review*, 39 (1), 5-23.

Harris, F. and de Chernatony, L. (2001), Corporate Branding and Corporate Brand Performance, *European Journal of Management, 35(3/4)*, 441.

Hatch, M.J. and Schultz, M. (2009), Of Bricks and Brands: From Corporate to Enterprise Branding, *Organizational Dynamics, 38(2)*, 117-130.

Hollensen, S. (2007), *Global Marketing*, Edinburgh: Pearson Education Limited.

Johnson, M. (2002), The Global Search for Talent Gets Tougher, *Financial Executive*, 18(4), 42-44.

Lenaghan, J.A. and Eisner, A.B. (2006), Employers of Choice and Competitive Advantage: The Proof is in the Pudding, *Organizational Culture, Communication and Conflict*, 10, 99-109.

Mackes, M. (2005), Becoming an Employer of Choice, *ASHRAE Journal*, 47, 59-60.

Melin, E. (2005), Employer Branding: Likenesses and Differences between External and internal employer brand images. Master's Thesis, Luleå University of Technology, MSc. Programmes in Engineering, Department of Business Administration and Social Sciences Division of Industrial Marketing and E-Commerce.

Minchington, B. (2006). *Your Employer Brand–Attract, Engage, Retain,* Australia: Collective Learning Australia.

Schultz, M. and de Chernatony, L. (2002), The Challenges of Corporate Branding, *Corporate Reputation Review*, *5(2/3)*, 105-112.

Sullivan, J. (2004), "*Eight Elements of a Successful Employment Brand*", ER Daily, 23 cited in Backhaus, K., and Tikoo, S. (2004), "*Conceptualizing and Researching Employer Branding*",

Career Development International, Vol. 9, No. 4/5, pp. 501-517.

Zivnuska, S., Ketchen, D.J. and Snow, C.C. (2001), Implications of the Converging Economy for Human Resource Management, *Research in Personnel and Human Resources Management, 20*, pp. 371-405.

12

Strategic Human Resources Management (SHRM)

Sumathi, G.N., T.J. Kamalanabhan and M. Thenmozhi

Introduction

Strategic human resource management (SHRM), in the recent times is addressed both by theorists and practitioners. Any research work on SHRM has to basically discuss how SHRM is more important than human resource management (HRM). A simple way to understand SHRM is: it is HRM in a macro perspective. Researchers have pointed that scientific evidence which is contextual in nature is part of the problem (Johns, 1993) but in the recent times, research in HRM takes context more seriously and frequently. (Begin, 1991) HRM is used as a term that encompasses: (a) specific human resource practices such as recruitment, selection and appraisal (b) formal human resource policies, which directly and partially constrain the development of specific practices, and (c) overarching human resource philosophies, which specify the values that inform an organization's policies and practices. (Jackson and Schuler, 1995)

In a simpler way, HRM is a system that attracts, develops, motivates and retains employees who ensure effective functioning and survival of the organization and its members. The two context of HRM include internal and external to the organization. The internal context of HRM includes technology, structure, size, organizational lifecycle stage and business strategy. While the external contextual factors include legal, social and political environments, unionization, labour market conditions, industry characteristics and national cultures. As organizational culture is bound to HRM, it is not looked separately. This paper considers strategy as a contextual factor and tries to study the HRM practices carried out in a firm. This article is based on the theme that HRM can help organizations' to achieve competitive advantage by lowering costs, by increasing sources of product and service differentiation or both (Porter, 1985) through human resources.

Linkages between HRM and Firm's Strategy

The fundamental reasons for integrating human resource management with strategic choice are: (a) to provide a broader range of solutions for solving complex organizational problems, (b) to ensure that human, financial and technological resources are considered in goal setting and capability assessment, (c) to explicitly consider individuals who are involved and to implement policies, and (d) to limit subordination of strategic considerations to human resource preferences and to limit the neglect of human resources as a vital source of organizational competence and competitive advantage. (Schuler and MacMillian, 1984) The present study tries to understand HRM in strategic context.

Researchers have described human resource strategy as a match between certain strategic or organizational conditions and certain specified aspects of human resource processes or skills. (Leontiades, 1982) In one approach, managerial skills and interests are matched with product or market environment assuming that environment will change very slowly. In other study, diagnosis of the business situation in terms of product life cycle helped to match executive characteristics to situational requirements. (Gerstein and Reisman, 1983) Yet another study, focused on expansion strategy (Leontiades, 1982) rather than product life cycles, where vertical integration, related diversification, or global expansion are given importance rather than emerging, growing and maturing product life cycles.

An alternate approach looked at matching firm's human

resource policies and processes with specific strategic choices (Smith, 1982a) and pointed the need to consider human resources management function tailored to reflect the future needs along with financial, marketing and technical plans. A study on compensation mix comprising of base pay, incentives and benefits showed that the compensation mix should be constructed for each phase of the firm's expansion cycle thereby offering a specific solution and not sufficiently comprehensive to influence total human resource strategy of the firm. Therefore, a study of HRM in strategic context is imperative.

Understanding SHRM

In order to understand SHRM, it is vital to understand the distinction between HRM and SHRM. The field of HRM consists of various practices used to manage people in organizations and these practices are grouped into sub disciplines of selection, training, appraisal and rewards. (Fombrum et al., 1984) These sub-disciplines possess little coordination among themselves as there are evolved from a micro-perspective that focuses only on a particular HR function. This lack of integration across the various HR activities paved researchers to make various attempts that focused on tying each functional area to the firm's strategy independent of other activities which finally resulted in the development of strategic selection, strategic appraisal, strategic development and strategic rewards. (Fombrum et al., 1984; Galgraith and Nathanson, 1979)

These attempts broadened the perspective of HRM by recognizing the need for each individual function to be aligned with organizational goals, even though the interplay between all of the functions is relatively neglected. (Lengnick- Hall and Lengnick Hall, 1988; Wright and Snell, 1991) Recently, the area of HRM is approached from a macro- perspective called as SHRM. (Butler et al., 1991) Hence in SHRM, the HRM functions are not only tied to the organizational goals but coordinated among themselves.

Miller (1987) defines SHRM practices as those decisions and actions which concern the management of employees at all levels in the business and which are related to the implementation of strategies directed towards sustaining competitive advantage. Guest (1989) suggested that SHRM is concerned with ensuring that human resources management is fully integrated into strategic planning; that HRM policies cohere both across policy areas and across hierarchies and that HRM practices are accepted and used by line managers as part of their everyday work. Wright and Snell (1991) considered SHRM to be organizational system designed to achieve sustainable competitive advantage through people. Ulrich and Lake (1991) described SHRM as a process of linking HR practices to business strategy.

Wright and McMahan (1992) considered SHRM as the pattern of planned HR deployments and activities intended to enable a firm achieve its goals. Truss and Gratton (1994) considered both process and outcome and defined SHRM as the linkage of HR functions with strategic goals and organizational objectives to improve business performance and cultivate an organizational culture that fosters innovation and flexibility.

Moreover, Bamberger and Meshoulam (2000) argued that SHRM is a competency-based approach to personnel management that focuses on the development of durable, imperfectly imitable and non-tradable people resources. Schuler and Walker (1990) referred human resource strategy to a short-term focus on business needs and defined it as a set of processes and activities jointly shared by human resources and line-managers to solve people-related business problems. However, in the absence of consistent definition, the central feature of SHRM involves designing and implementing a set of internally consistent policies and practices to ensure that firm's human capital contributes to achieving business objectives. (Gratton and Hope-Hailey, 1999; Jackson and

Schuler, 1995)

Writers in the area of SHRM have focused on: (a) human resource accounting, that assigns value to human resources in an effort to quantify the organizational capacity (Flamholtz, 1985), (b) human resource planning (Baird et al. 1983), (c) responses to strategic change in the environment (Fombrun, 1982), (d) matching human resources to strategic or organizational conditions (Leontiades, 1982), in which recruitment, selection and retention (Galosy, 1983); compensation systems, domain choice (Miles and Snow, 1978); productivity (Deutch, 1982) and other specific elements are examined, and (e) broader scope of human resource strategies. (Dyer, 1984) In a basic sense, SHRM integrates HRM with strategy of the organization.

What has happened to IBM when it hired programmers from outside, taught them programming skills and made the programmers aware of their own, the customer's needs and corporate climate? (Schuler and MacMillan, 1984) The customer gained strong ties with IBM and IBM gains strong ties with programmers that ultimately blocked certain career paths for programmers and finally raised the switching costs of IBM though improving the firm's competitive position. In IBM's case, the integration of HRM practices with competitive strategy of low switching cost on the long run become uncertain. In spite of these difficulties, firms desire to integrate human resource management with strategic choice to achieve competitive advantage through people. The theoretical perspectives behind firm's achieving competitive advantage through people and firm's HRM link with strategy encompass role behaviour perspective, institutional/resource dependence theory, resource based theory and agency/transaction cost theory and cybernetic system.

Resource-based View of the Firm

The resource based view of the firm is based on the link between strategy and the internal resources of the firm.

According to RBV, it is fundamental to understand competitive advantage and sustained competitive advantage. Firms achieve competitive advantage, when it is implementing a value creating strategy not simultaneously being implemented by any current or potential competitors and a sustained competitive advantage exists only after efforts to replicate that advantage have ceased. (Barney, 1991) According RBV of the firm, competitive advantage can occur only when firm has resource heterogeneity and resource immobility. Firm resource heterogeneity refers to the physical capital, human capital and organizational capital of the firm that varies across different firms.

Firm resource immobility refers to the inability of the competing firm to obtain resources of other firms. The four criteria for a firm to provide sustained competitive advantage are the resources which: (a) must add value, (b) must be unique or rare, (c) must be imperfectly imitable, and (d) cannot be substituted. Firms capitalize on human resource management s a means of gaining and maintaining competitive advantage. (Schuler and MacMillan, 1984) While describing human resources as competitive advantage, Ulrich (1991) partially relied on resource based theoretical perspective of the firm and expanded Porter's (1985) model of competitive advantage to include organizational culture, distinctive competence and strategic unity as mediators in the strategy-competitive advantage link. He discussed how human resource practices can be used by firms to develop strategies that will lead to sustained competitive advantage, stating that there must be a focus on the relationship between human resources, strategies and competitive advantage.

Behavioural Perspective

The behavioural perspective has its roots in contingency theory (Fisher, 1989) that focuses on the employee behaviour as a mediator between strategy and firm performance. Based on this theory, various employment practices are carried out to elicit and control employee attitude and behaviours. The specific attitudes behaviours would vary across organizations based on the organizational strategy. According to the behavioural perspective, employee role behaviours are instrumental in the implementation of the competitive strategies. Jackson and Schuler (1987) have proposed three competitive strategies: innovation, quality enhancement and cost reduction that would elicit respective employee role behaviours. Schuler (1992) builds upon behavioural perspective and proposed that the specific HR practices that motivate employees to exhibit the needed role behaviours are associated with various strategies. He also stresses that all of the HRM activities must be consistent with each other and in turn linked to the strategic needs of the business.

Miles and Snow (1984) described HR practices that are required for different strategy types: defenders, prospectors and reactors with the assumption that HR practices differ among strategy types due to the different behaviours and skills necessary to carry out the strategy.

Cybernetic Systems

Cybernetic models vary in the treatment of the systems: closed system like behavioural perspective (Thompson, 1967) and open system being open to exchanges with their environment. (Katz and Kahn, 1978) In the open systems model, input in the HR system are the competencies of the individual in the firm, throughput process is the behaviour of those individuals in the organizational system and the output consists of performance and affective outcomes. (Wright and Snell, 1991) The major focus of Wright and Snell model was on the coordination of various HR practices across sub-functions like selection, appraisal, compensation, training etc. and the alignment of various HR practices to some strategic end rather than simply focusing on how one set of practices supports a firm's strategy. Snell (1992) combined cybernetic systems and behavioural perspective to term as control theory view of SHRM. He proposed that the control process includes superior intentions, influence mechanisms and evaluation and feedback and combined HRM practices into three types of control systems: (a) behavioural control, (b) output control, and (c) input control.

Agency/Transaction Cost Theory

Transaction costs are the costs associated with negotiating, monitoring, evaluating and enforcing exchanges between parties and they are incurred in order to make exchanges more efficient. Agency costs are the costs associated with establishing efficient contract between parties. (Jensen and Meckling, 1976) As agency/transaction cost theory seeks to explain control in organizations, they have implications for the design of HRM practices. (Jones, 1984) The role of HRM practices is to allow for the measurement of unique contributions and to provide unique rewards for employee performance, as they are means through firms are able to align employee behaviour with the strategic goals of the organization.

Resource Dependence/Institutional Theory

Resource dependence/institutional theory focuses on the relationship between an organization and its constituencies. Institutional theory concerns about social acceptability and legitimacy (Pfeffer and Cohen, 1984) while the resource dependence theory emphasizes resource exchanges as the key feature of these relationships.

According to resource dependence theory, organizational gain power over each other by controlling values resources. For example, personnel department exerts power over the other departments by controlling the flow of human resources into and through the organization. (Pfeffer and Cohen, 1984)

Competitive Strategies of a Firm

Competitive strategy is about being different as it

deliberately chooses a different set of activities to deliver a unique mix of value. Strategic initiative is crucial for firm's growth and prosperity in order to gain and retain competitive advantage. Strategic initiative is the ability to capture control of strategic behaviour in the industries in which a firm competes. (Schuler and MacMillan, 1984) The concept of competitive advantage is described as the essence of competitive strategy. (Porter, 1980) Porter has described three strategies to gain competitive advantage: innovation, quality enhancement and cost reduction. Innovation strategy is used to develop products or services different from those of competitors, where the primary focus is to offer something new and different. The primary focus of quality enhancement strategy is to enhance product or service quality. In the cost reduction strategy, firms attempt to gain competitive advantage by offering the lowest cost product.

The basic reason behind linking competitive strategies with HRM is to get a desired role employee behaviour required to perform a specific task. (Schneider, 1985)

Linking Quality Enhancement Strategy with HRM

At Xerox, CEO David Kearns defines quality as "being right the first time every time". According to James Houghton, Chairman of Corning Glass Works, his company's total quality approach is about people. At Corning, good ideas come from employees for which workers formed a quality circles to solved work related problems. The sales of L.L. Beans have increased tenfold while the number of permanent employees has grown only five-fold. (Prokesh, 1985) The present article considers quality enhancement strategy as the competitive strategy of the organization and tries to link this strategy with HRM to bring out needed role behaviour. The profile of employee behaviours necessary for firms to pursue a strategy of quality enhancement (Schuler and Jackson, 1995) is mentioned below:

1. Relatively repetitive and predictable behaviours.

2. A more long-term or intermediate focus.
3. A modest amount of cooperative, interdependent behaviour.
4. A high concern for quality.
5. A modest concern for quantity of output.
6. High concern for process (how the goods or services are made or delivered).
7. Low risk-taking activity.
8. Commitment to the goals of the organization.

Schuler (1988) has given human resource management practices that are needed to link with competitive strategies. In Table 12.1, human resource management practice menus are shown that covers the aspects of planning, staffing, appraising, compensating and training and development.

Table 12.1: Human Resource Management Practice Menus

	Planning Choices	
Informal	-	Formal
Short-term	-	Long-term
Explicit job analysis	-	Implicit job analysis
Job simplification	-	Job enrichment
Low employee involvement	-	High employee involvement
	Staffing Choices	
Internal sources	-	External sources
Narrow paths	-	Broad paths
Single ladder	-	Multiple ladders
Explicit criteria	-	Implicit criteria
Limited socialization	-	Extensive socialization
Closed procedures	-	Open procedures
Appraising choices		
Behavioural criteria	-	Results criteria
	Purposes: Development, Remedial, Maintenance	
Low employee participation	-	High employee participation
Short-term criteria	-	Long-term criteria
Individual criteria	-	Group criteria

Contd...

Compensating Choices		
Low base salaries	-	High base salaries
Internal equity	-	External equity
Few perks	-	Many perks
Standard, fixed package	-	Flexible package
Low participation	-	High participation
No incentives	-	Many incentives
Short-term incentives	-	Long-term incentives
No employment security	-	High employment security
Hierarchical	-	High participation
Training and Development		
Short-term	-	Long-term
Narrow application	-	Broad application
Productivity emphasis	-	Quality of work life emphasis
Spontaneous, unplanned	-	Planned, systematic
Individual orientation	-	Group orientation
Low participation	-	High participation

Source: Adapted from Schuler, R.S. "Human Resources Management Practice Choices", in Schuler, R.S., S.A. Youngblood and V.L. Huber (eds.) *Readings in Personnel and Human Resource Management*, 3rd edition, St. Paul, MN: West Publishing, 1988.

Schuler and Jackson (1995) have offered a set of hypotheses based on the descriptions of quality enhancement strategy and the role behaviour and the brief typology of HRM practices. In order to gain competitive advantage through quality enhancement strategy, the key HRM practices include

1. Relatively fixed and explicit job descriptions.
2. High levels of employee participation in decisions relevant to immediate work conditions and the job itself.
3. A mix of individual and group criteria for performance appraisal.
4. Performance appraisal that is mostly short-term and result oriented.
5. Relatively egalitarian treatment of employees and some guarantees of employment security.

6. Extensive and continuous training and development of employees.

Based on the above discussion, the following propositions are made:

1. The HRM practices of the firms pursing quality enhancement strategy will have clear job descriptions.
2. The HRM practices of the firms pursing quality enhancement strategy will include high levels of employee participation in decisions regarding work conditions.
3. The HRM practices of the firms pursing quality enhancement strategy will include high levels of employee participation in decisions regarding job.
4. The firms pursing quality enhancement strategy will carry out performance appraisal based on a mix of individual and group criteria.
5. The performance appraisal will be for a short-term among the firms pursing quality enhancement strategy.
6. The performance appraisal will be result oriented among the firms pursing quality enhancement strategy.
7. The employees will be treated equally among the firms pursing quality enhancement strategy.
8. The firms pursing quality enhancement strategy will guarantee employment security.
9. Training will be planned and systematic among the firms pursing quality enhancement strategy.
10. Continuous training and development programs will be carried out in the firms pursing quality enhancement strategy.

Scope for Future Research

The propositions can be studied and empirically tested among the firms, in order to ensure the alignment of HRM practices with quality enhancement strategy. The other two competitive strategies such as innovation strategy and cost reduction strategy could also be tested in a similar way. The propositions of this paper are general that enables researchers to use these propositions in different contextual settings. In addition, this paper is focused towards HRM practices that are based on quality enhancement strategy with the basic assumption that the firms already carry out HRM activities to manage people.

References

Baird, L., Mesholum, L., and DeGive, G. (1983), Meshing Human Resources Planning with Strategic Business Planning: A Model Approach, *Personnel*, 60, 14-25.

Bamberger, P. and Meshoulam, I. (1988), *Human Resource Strategy: Formulation, Implementation and Impact,* Sage, Beverly Hills, CA.

Barney, J. (1991), Firm Resources and Sustained Competitive Advantage, *Journal of Management,* 17, 99-120.

Begin, J.P. (1991), *Strategic Employment Policy,* Englewood Cliffs, NJ: Prentice-Hall.

Deutch, A. (1982), How Employee Retention Strategies Can Aid Productivity, *Journal of Business Strategy,* 2, 106-109.

Dyer, L. (1984), Studying Human Resource Strategy: An Approach and an Agenda, *Industrial Relations,* 23, 156-169.

Fisher, C. (1989), Current and Recurrent Challenges in HRM, *Journal of Management,* 15,157-180.

Flamholtz, *Human Resource Accounting,* San Francisco: Jossey Bass, 1985.

Fombrun, C. (1982), Environmental Trends Create New Pressures on Human Resources, *Journal of Business Strategy*, 3, 61-69.

Fombrun, C.J., Tichy, N.M. and Devanna, M.A. (1984), *Strategic Human Resource Management,* New York: Wiley.

Galosy, J.R. (1983), Meshing Human Resources Planning with Strategic Business Planning: One Company's Experience, *Personnel,* 60, 26-35.

Gerstein, M. and Reisman, H. (1983), Strategic Selection: Matching Executives to Business Condition, *Sloan Management Review*, 24, 33-49.

Gratton, L. and Hope-Hailey, V. (1999), Linking Individual Performance to Business Strategy: The People Process Model, *Human Resource Management,* 38, 17-31.

Jackson, S.E. and Schuler, R.S. (1995), HRM in the Context of Organizations, *Annual Review of Psychology,* 46, 237-264.

Jensen, M. and W. Meckling (1976), Theory of the Firm: Managerial Behaviour, Agency Costs and Ownership Structure, *Journal of Financial Economics*, 3, 305-360.

Johns, G. (1993), Constraints on the Adoption of Psychology-based Personnel Practices: Lessons form Organization Innovation, *Personnel Psychology*, 46, 561-591.

Jones, G. (1984), Task Visibility, Free Riding and Shrinking: Explaining the Effect of Structure and Technology on Employee Behaviours, *Academy of Management Review*, 9, 684-695.

Katz, D. and Khan, R. (1978), *The Social Psychology of Organization,* New York, NY: John Wiley and Sons.

Leontiades, M. (1982), Choosing the Right Manager to Fit the Strategy, *Journal of Business Strategy,* 3, 58-69.

Miles, R. and C.C. Snow (1978), *Organizational Strategy, Structure and Process,* New York: McGraw Hill.

Miles, R. and C.C. Snow (1984), Designing Strategic Human Resource Systems, *Organizational Dynamics*, 13, 36-52.

Pfeffer, J. and Y. Cohen (1984), Determinants of Internal Labour Markets in Organizations, *Administrative Science Quarterly*, 29, 550-572.

Porter, M.E. (1985), *Competitive Advantage: Creating and Sustaining Superior Performance.* New York: Free Press.

Porter, M. E. (1980), *Competitive Strategy: Techniques for Analyzing Industries and Competitors.* New York: Free Press.

Prokesch, S. E. (1985), Bean Meshes Man, Machine, *The New York Times*, December 23, 19, 21.

13

Managing Diverse Workforce in the 21st Century

Sajeet Pradhan and Rabindra Kumar Pradhan

Introduction

Diversity has emerged an important issue because of imbalanced representation of diversity groups in the workforce. Diversity is more than just a passing management fad. Over the past few years it has become reason for competitive advantage for many organizations whereas there are many others who are yet to be convinced of its potent. The sceptics fail to recognize the merits associated with a vibrant and diverse workforce. Not just diverse workforce improves morale there is also rational monetary gain associated with people of different backgrounds. India is not only a diverse society, but also one which has valued and celebrated diversity. Indian culture is very well described by the term 'synergic pluralism' for the reason that it has embraced people of different beliefs into its social mainstream. (Pareek, 1992) India is the only country in the world to have reservations for underprivileged sections of the society to bring them back to the mainstream.

There are several reasons why diversity is such an important issue in India—first India has interesting statistics of highest number of millionaires cohabiting with highest number of poverty stricken people in the world. Secondly, there is enormous pressure by WTO and IBRD to have inclusive growth which involves large number of under-represented people. The objective of this chapter is to highlight the importance of diversity in a country like India and emphasizes how this diversity in workforce can provide sustainable competitive advantage to organizations. The article also highlights the challenges before the corporate world particularly Indian business houses which desire to spread their wings in global markets.

What is Diversity?

Diversity is dealing with a collective mixture of differences and similarities in a given group. Although there is no consensus about what diversity means, there's considerable agreement regarding the components of diversity. (Wentling and Palma-Rivas, 2000) There are several bases of diversity: demographic (age, gender, education), social (religion, language, region, caste, tribes, physical and mental handicaps), and ideological (different ways of perceiving issues). Another definition of diversity mentions the inclusion of age, education, background, function, and personality. It also includes lifestyles, sexual orientation, geographic origin, tenure with an organization, management and non-management values, beliefs, and opinions (Robbins, 2008).

Categories of Diversity

As mentioned above diversity includes several categories and characteristics. They are broadly subdivided into primary and secondary categories of diversity. Primary category includes genetic characteristics that affect a person's self-image and socialization, whereas, secondary category comprises learned characteristics that a person acquires and modifies throughout life.

The following are the brief explanations of the primary categories of diversity.

Age: It refers to the number of years a person has been alive or the generation into which the individual was born (veterans, baby boomers, xers and nexters).

Race: It means the biological groupings within the mankind, representing superficial physical differences, such as eye colour and skin colour. Race accounts for less than 1 percent of the difference in a person's genetic heredity.

Ethnicity: It refers to identification with a cultural group that has shared traditions and heritage, including nationality, language, religiosity, dietary habits, and customs.

Gender: It means biological sex as determined by female or male.

Physical Abilities and Qualities: A variety of characteristics, including body type, physical size, facial features, specific abilities or disabilities, and visible and invisible physical and mental talents or limitations.

Sexual Orientations: Feelings of sexual attraction toward members of the same or gender, such as heterosexual, homosexual, or bisexual.

The following are the brief explanations of the secondary categories of diversity.

Education: One's formal and informal learning and training.

Work Experience: The employment and volunteer positions the person has held and the variety of organizations for which the person has worked.

Income: The economic conditions in which the person grew up and his current economic status.

Marital Status: The person's situation as never married, married, widowed, or divorced.

Religious Beliefs: Fundamental teachings received about deities and values acquired from formal or informal religious practices.

Geographic Location: The location where the person was born or has spent considerable part of his or her life; it also includes types of communities like rural or urban.

Parental Status: It refers to whether the person has children or not. It also means the circumstances under which children are raised such as single parenting or two-adult parenting.

Personal Style: It means the tendency of the individual to think, feel, or act in a particular way.

Another classification of diversity is surface-level

diversity and deep-level diversity. (Taylor, 1993) Surface-level diversity includes observable demographic or physiological differences in people, such as their race, ethnicity, gender, age, and physical disabilities. Whereas deep-level diversity refers to the difference in the psychological characteristics of employees, including personalities, beliefs, values, and attitudes.

Workforce Diversity in India

India is a country of interesting contradictions. India is a multicultural, multi-religion, multi-linguistic, and multi-caste society. Indian social system has been traditionally based on the caste system. People from various neighbouring countries like Nepal, Bhutan, Bangladesh, Tibet, and Sri Lanka have migrated into India and stayed here for better life and job prospects. India harbours all the major faiths in the world. It is the birthplace of many religions like Hinduism, Buddhism, Jainism, and Sikhism. People from diverse faiths live harmoniously and tolerantly.

India has largest number of millionaires and has the dubious distinction of having largest number of poor people (people below poverty line).We have super malls, five star hotels sharing space with the largest slum in Asia (Dharavi). By opening of economy to the outside world and by becoming member of WTO (World Trade Organization), India has created opportunities for its young population to amass wealth. According to a recent report, while the past decade saw the bulk of IT workforce are Indians, the present decade will see nearly 20 percent of the workforce to be non-Indians. Whereas in coming future Indian companies will migrate to domain specific services from the current delivery-centric activities.

As we discuss the diversity of workforce in India and its impact on business in particular and society in general, there are several organizations which have started in this direction. Tata Consultancy Services (TCS) has more than 2 lakh employees belonging to more than 40 countries. It has software development centres in nine countries outside India. Another Indian IT giant, Infosys has 63 offices and development centres in more than 30 countries. Tata Motors have 950 non-Indian employees out of total employee strength of 22,000.Ranbaxy Laboratories has 1600 global employees out of a total employee strength of 10,000; one-fourth of its managerial talent, including its ex-CEO Brian Tempest. Bharat Forge has all its country managers of foreign origin.

The demographic profile in India is changing very fast. Lot of youngsters are entering the workforce. Spread of education, legislation, and social movements has brought significant changes in workforce composition. In present decade, more women have entered into corporate world than the previous decades. Members of minority community are given preference through legislation so as to bridge the gap between the privileged section of the society and the lesser privileged ones.

Diversity is important at all levels. While in many organizations it is confined to lower levels (workers and office staff), in other it is all pervasive that is spread to the upper echelon. One diversity issue in India is the ratio of women executives at different levels of an organization. A CII study has revealed that the attrition among the women workers is that of 7 percent against a whopping 59 percent in case of male workers. Yet, only 45 percent women reach the junior management level, and only 2 percent become senior managers. Indian organizations have to accommodate a very diverse social group of employees, based on varying socio-economic, ethnic, and linguistic composition (Robbins and Sanghi, 2005). The Constitution of India has determined the following categories:

1. Scheduled castes (SCs) and scheduled tribes (STs).
2. Other backward castes (OBCs).
3. Bonafide members of the State.
4. Ex-defence and paramilitary personnel.
5. Disabled personnel.

6. Displaced personnel.
7. Gender issues.
8. Age factor.
9. Temporary/casual workers.

Diversity as a Source of Competitive Advantage

Managing diversity may look like a contradiction within itself. It means being precisely aware of characteristics common to a group of employees, while also managing these employees as individuals. (Johnston, 1991) It is not just about tolerating or accommodating all kinds of differences arising out of diverse backgrounds and divergent expectations but supporting, encouraging and utilizing these differing points of view to a firm's advantage. (Luthans, 2002)

Organizations can convert the confusing motley of multicultural, multi-religious, multiethnic, multiregional workforce into its competitive advantage. For example, Longo Toyota in El Monte, California, has built its competitive strategy on that idea. With a 60-person sales-force that speaks more than 20 languages, Longo's staff provides a considerable competitive advantage for catering to an increasingly diverse customer base. (Gilbert and Ivancevich, 2000)

Diversity can provide sustainable competitive advantage to a firm in following ways:

1. By helping an organisation in gaining and retaining market share.
2. Through significant cost savings.
3. Through increased productivity and innovation.
4. Providing better quality management.
5. Enhancing organisational flexibility.

Diversity an Impossible Challenge

Despite a general awareness in organisations about the positivity of diversity, both individuals and organisations find it difficult in accepting diversity in workplace. (Jackson, 1992) People belonging to homogeneous backgrounds are especially vulnerable to attitudes that prevent them from being more open to diversity—both in the workplace and in their personal lives. There are several barriers that prevent us from accepting diversity. These include:

1. **Prejudice:** A person's unjustified attitude towards another person based on his or her membership of a particular group or community.
2. **Ethnocentrism:** It's a tendency to consider one's group, race, culture, language, region, religion, or nation as superior to others. Individuals who are ethnocentric see their group-related customs or beliefs as 'right' and evaluate other, beliefs or practices against that yardstick.
3. **Stereotypes:** This refers to set of beliefs about a group that is applied universally to all members of that group, such as 'people from South are good in English" or "people from North-East states are poor". Stereotyping, whether positive or negative, is not good because seldom does one statement hold true for all members of a group.
4. **Discrimination:** It means barring an individual from membership of an organisation or from a job because of his or her membership of a particular group. An example of discrimination in workplace is the preference of male employees over female employees for work which requires lots of travelling.
5. **Harassment:** It means conscious shunning or verbally or physically abusing an individual because of his or her membership of a particular group.
6. **Sexual Harassment:** It is one of the most toxic workplace behaviours. It refers to all kind of unwanted, uninvited, and intimate overtures towards one by others which is sexually motivated.
7. **Backlash:** It refers to negative reaction to gaining of power and influence by members of previously under-represented groups, leading to fear, resentment, and reverse discrimination.

Managing Diversity Effectively

Managing diversity effectively is one of the top priorities of managers in all organizations—large and small, public and private, for profit or not for profit. (Thomas, 1990) Managers need to ensure that they and their subordinates appreciate the value that diversity brings to an organization and understand why diversity should be celebrated rather than ignored. Managers have the onus to create an environment where people interact freely and work effectively with men and women who are physically challenged or are of diverse race, age, gender, ethnicity, cultural values, nationality, or sexual orientation. (Fernandez and Barr, 1993)

There are several ways diversity can be effectively managed and made part of organizational ethos, ways like:

Awareness Building: Awareness demands appreciation of diversity as a fact of organizational life. Certain proactive companies are developing awareness campaigns to help employees understand the pain and indignity of harassment. Awareness building is designed to increase awareness of the meaning and importance of valuing diversity. The major aim is to sensitize employees to the assumption they make about others and the way those assumptions affect their behaviours, decisions and judgement.

Diversity Training and Skill Building: Diversity training and skill building programs attempt to identify and reduce hidden biases and to contribute in a constructive manner towards the goals of a multicultural, multiethnic group. The training will help employees learn about the similarities and difference they have with other team members or organisational members. They are taught to appreciate and be tolerant towards differing opinions and values. Companies like Motorola offers language training to their employees so as to bridge the gap between people of different communities.

Many diversity awareness programs often the following goals:

1. Providing organisation members with accurate information

on diversity.

2. Revealing personal biases and stereotypes which are generally unknown to employees.
3. Assessing personal beliefs, attitudes, and values, and learning about other points of view.
4. Dismissing or refuting inaccurate stereotypes and beliefs about different groups.
5. Creating and supporting an environment in which people feel free to share their differing perspectives and points of view.
6. Improving understanding of others who are different from oneself.

Communications: Opening avenues of communication so that people of different backgrounds and mindsets can interact with each other in a candid and honest way. One top expert on diverse workforce states that 90 percent of all problems can be resolved through open and honest communication. Organisations across the globe understand this and design their orientation sessions in such a fashion that employees from various and varied background can feel comfortable working with each other. To this end, managers must encourage open communication among young and old employees, workers, minorities, disabled, etc. This way everyone will learn about other's personal values and beliefs.

Encourage Feedback: Feedback is one way by which it can be judged how the person wants to be treated. This will greatly help managers dealing with heterogeneous team. Feedback about harassment, especially sexual harassment, will help in curbing this nuisance from its very root. The complainant's identity should be kept secret so as any unwarranted backlash by the accused can be avoided and employees belonging to any minority can feel protected and safe.

Organisational Practices: Several organisations have come up with flexible working schedules and job arrangements so as to accommodate diversity in their workforce. Religious festivals, cultural events, may be accommodated in a flexible manner, keeping both individuals and groups in mind. Various HR practices can be designed and implemented in a way which will adjust organisational diversity.

Commitment of the Top Management: When there is honest and unflinching commitment of top management towards diversity the message percolates down to the bottom layers. Many diversity management programs have failed because of the indifferent treatment it has received by top management. A policy of zero tolerance towards harassment and ill treatment of people of other background will deter employees to tread such path.

Promoting Diversity through Pluralism

Pluralism refers to an environment in which individual differences are acknowledged, appreciated and seen as significant contributors to the entirety. (Galagan, 1991) A diverse workforce is most effective when managers are capable of guiding the organisation towards achieving pluralism. According to Jim Kim, there are five specific approaches that can help organisation achieve this:

1. **Golden Rule Approach:** "Do unto others as you would have them do unto you". This is a universal rule preaching morality. However, people apply the rule from their own frame without understanding the cultural expectations, traditions, and preferences of the other individual.
2. **Assimilation Approach:** This aims at shaping organisation members to fit the existing culture. The dominant culture makes others follow it without failure.
3. **Righting the Wrongs Approach:** According to this approach the past injustices suffered by a particular group will be corrected, paving the way for career mobility and career success. This approach tries to compensate for the damages a particular group has suffered because of historical inequities.
4. **Culture Specific Approach:** It refers to learning the

nuances of another culture when the employee is assigned responsibility in a foreign country.

5. **Multicultural Approach:** This approach gives employees the opportunity to develop an appreciation for both differences of culture and variations in personal characteristics. It is a very effective way of achieving pluralism since it advocates change on the part of management, employees, and organisation systems and practices.

Conclusion

Diversity is highly critical subject in a multilayered and multicultural society like India. Today, Indian organizations have become truly global as they are acquiring multinational assets, investing huge money in foreign projects, hiring foreign nationals for their foreign assignments in such circumstances Indian organizations should set benchmark in managing and harnessing the potential of diverse workforce. Although there are many challenges like stereotypes, past practices, jingoism, biased opinions that has to be overcome to convert diversity into sustainable competitive advantage. Diversity can be managed and made part of the mainstream in several ways like, through creating awareness, imparting diversity training and skill building, through organizational practices, by facilitating open communication and creating avenues to provide feedback and lastly by the support of the top management. Diversity can also be managed effectively through pluralism. There are multiple advantages to a diverse workforce which once realized will give fillip to the organizational reputation and boost to its very revenue.

References

Bradford, S. (1996), Fourteen Dimensions of Diversity: Understanding and Appreciating Differences in the Workplace, in J. W. Pfeiffer (ed.), 1996 Annual Volume (2), *Consulting*, San Diego: Pfeiffer and Associates, 9-17.

Fernandez, J.P. and Barr, M. (1993), *The Diversity Advantage*, New

York: Lexington Books.

Galagan, P.A. (1991), Tapping the Power of Diverse Workforce, *Training and Development Journal*, 45(3), 38-44.

Gilbert, J.A. and Ivancevich, J.M. (2000), Valuing Diversity: A Tale of Two Organisations. *Academy of Management Executive*, 14(1), 93-105.

Jackson, S.E. (1992), *Diversity in the Workplace,* New York: Guildford.

Johnston, W.B. (1991), Global Workforce 2000: The New World Labour Market, Harvard Business Review, 69(2), 115-127.

Luthans, F. (2002), *Organisational Behaviour,* New York: McGraw Hill.

Pareek, U. (1992), Coercive and Persuasive Power Scale, *Indian Journal of Industrial Relations*, 30 (2), 175-189.

Robbins, S.P. (2008), *Organisational Behaviour,* Engelwood Cliffs, NJ: Prentice Hall.

Robbins, S.P. and Sanghi, S. (2005), *Organisational Behaviour,* New Delhi: Pearson Education.

Taylor, C. (1993), *Cultural Diversity in Organisations,* San Francisco: Berrett-Kochler.

Thomas, R. (1990), From Affirmative Action to Affirming Diversity, *Harvard Business Review*, 68(2), 107-117.

Wentling, R.M. and Palma-Rivas, N. (2000), Current Status of Diversity Initiatives in Selected Multinational Corporations, *Human Resource Development Quarterly*, 11 (1), 35-60.

14

Workforce Diversity: Challenges and Best Practices

Ansumalini Panda

One of the most basic challenges currently faced by organizations is how to accommodate people of different kinds. This is also a big challenge for effectiveness of globalization. Once upon a time, workforce diversity was an important issue for an organization to address the differences among its people within a given country. Now it has become a global concern. Managing diversity at work is ideally driven by corporate strategy or mission so that employees and their organization can benefit from it. Thus, it is important to understand the theoretical concept and realize its practical applications for managing today's organizations.

Concept of Diversity

According to Thomas (1992,) dimensions of workplace diversity include, but are not limited to, age, ethnicity, ancestry, gender, physical abilities/qualities, race, sexual orientation, educational background, geographic location, income, marital status, military experience, religious beliefs, parental status, and work experience.

Diversity represents the multitude of individual differences that exists among people. Work force diversity is a function of the similarities and differences among employees in such characteristics as age, gender, ethnic heritage, physical ability or disability, race and sexual orientation. Diversity in the workplace is growing faster than we can address its concomitant issues. Constant changes in a firm's culture and in people's personal belief's force the workplace to deal with the concept and issue of diversity. Managing employee heterogeneity is more important and more difficult than managing homogeneity in fully utilizing internal human resources.

Thomas (1995), defines diversity as any mixture of components characterized by similarities and differences. The components of a diversity mixture include differences and similarities between and among races, ages, genders, educational levels, religious affiliations, geographical origins, and work styles.

In general, diversity can be regarded as the broad spectrum of variation that distinguishes among the human resources of an organization. This multidimensional view of diversity assumes that humans differ from one another along any number of dimensions. Whereas some dimensions are highly visible (i.e. race and gender), other are less so (i.e. values, personality, education, experience, sexual orientation, and religion).

Managing Diversity

Managing diversity focuses on building diversity management related skills and changing policies or strategies. Managing diversity entails enabling people to perform up to their maximum potential. It focuses on changing the organization culture and infrastructure such that people provide the highest productivity possible. Effectively managing diversity can influence the organizations costs and employee attitudes, recruitment of human resources, sales and market share, creativity and innovation, group problem solving and productivity.

As suggested by Thomas (1992) and Cox (1993), there are several best practices that a HR manager can adopt in ensuring effective management of workplace diversity in order to attain organizational goals. They are as follows:

1. **Mentoring:** Initiating a diversity mentoring program is one of the most effective ways to deal with. This could

entail involving different departmental managers in a mentoring program to coach and provide feedback to employees who are different from them. In order for the program to run successfully, it is wise to provide practical training for the managers or seek help from consultants and experts in this field. Usually, such a program will encourage organization's members to air their opinions and learn how to resolve conflict due to their diversity. More importantly, the purpose of a diversity mentoring program seeks to encourage members to move beyond their own culture frame of reference to recognize and take full advantage of the productivity potential inherent in a diverse population.

2. **Organizing Talents Strategically:** As more and more companies are going for their market expansions either physically or virtually (for example, commerce related companies), there is a necessity to employ diverse talents to understand the various niches of the market. For example, when China was opening up its market and exporting their products globally in the late 1980s, the Chinese companies (China's electronic giants such as Haier) were seeking the marketing expertise of Singaporeans. This is because Singapore's marketing talents are able to understand local China market relatively well.
3. **Leading the Talk:** A HR manager needs to advocate a diverse workforce by making diversity evident at all organizational levels. Otherwise some employees will quickly conclude that there is no future for them in the company. As a HR manager, it is pertinent to show respect for diversity issues and promote clear and positive responses to them. He/she must also show a high level of commitment and be able to resolve issues of workplace diversity in ethical and responsible manner.
4. **Control and Measure Results:** A HR manager must conduct regular organizational assessment issues like pay,

benefits, work environment, management and promotional opportunities to assess the progress over the long-term. There is also need to develop appropriate measuring tools to measure the impact of diversity initiatives at the organizations, through organization-wide feedback surveys and other methods.

5. **Motivational Approach:** Workplace motivation can be defined as the influence that makes us do things to achieve organizational goals, this is result of our individuals needs being satisfied so that we are motivated to complete organizational tasks effectively. As these needs vary from person to person, an organization must be able to utilize different motivational tools to encourage their employees to put in the required effort and increase productivity for the company.

Challenges

As with anything that requires a change in established attitudes and behaviour, achieving true diversity in the workplace can be a challenge. The challenges of diversity in the workplace are often the result of a combination of different factors, but resistance to change on the part of both employees and employers continues to be the primary underlying issue. Due to policies like affirmative action and an increasing trend among employers to promote diversity in the workplace and expand their hiring channels and methods, diversity in many forms within the corporate world is more common today than in previous decades. Everyone however, does not always view exposure to races, cultures, and beliefs that differ widely from their own, as a positive thing. As such, the challenges of diversity in the workplace reflect this. Some common challenges and issues are mentioned below.

1. **Communication:** Without proper communication, barriers that exist between groups of people due to actual or perceived differences and pre-conceived notions cannot be effectively broken down. The purpose of diversity training

in the workplace, among other things, is to improve communications between diverse social groups. Perceptual, cultural and language barriers need to be overcome for diversity programs to succeed. Ineffective communication of key objectives results in confusion, lack of teamwork, and low morale.

2. **Resistance to Change:** There are always employees who will refuse to accept the fact that the social and cultural makeup of their workplace is changing. The "we've always done it this way" mentality silences new ideas and inhibits progress.
3. **Implementation of Diversity in the Workplace Policies:** This can be the overriding challenge to all diversity advocates. Armed with the results of employee assessments and research data, they must build and implement a customized strategy to maximize the effects of diversity in the workplace for their particular organization.
4. **Successful Management of Diversity in the Workplace:** Diversity training alone is not sufficient for one's organization's diversity management plan. A strategy must be created and implemented to create a culture of diversity that permeates every department and function of the organization.

Diversity Management

Related to the challenge of policy implementation, diversity management must be properly delegated and enforced in order to be effective. If no one person or department is in charge of enforcement and implementation of any type of policy, it goes without saying that the policy will most likely not be effectively followed or enforced. Creating a more diverse workplace should be the goal of every company and its employees as well. While overcoming existing attitudes and beliefs concerning others may be difficult, the resulting benefits, including a more dynamic workplace and an environment where everyone feels accepted and valued for their contributions far outweigh the costs of leaving established comfort zones.

An organization's success and competitiveness depends upon its ability to embrace diversity and realize the benefits. When organizations actively assess their handling of workplace diversity issues, develop and implement diversity plans, multiple benefits are reported such as the following.

Organizations employing a diverse workforce can supply a greater variety of solutions to problems in service, sourcing, and allocation of resources. Employees from diverse backgrounds bring individual talents and experiences in suggesting ideas that are flexible in adapting to fluctuating markets and customer demands.

A diverse collection of skills and experiences (e.g. languages, cultural understanding) allows a company to provide service to customers on a global basis.

A diverse workforce that feels comfortable communicating varying points of view provides a larger pool of ideas and experiences. The organization can draw from that pool to meet business strategy needs and the needs of customers more effectively.

Companies that encourage diversity in the workplace inspire all of their employees to perform to their highest ability. Company-wide strategies can then be executed; resulting in higher productivity, profit, and return on investment.

Recommended Steps

Assessment of Diversity in the Workplace: Top companies make assessing and evaluating their diversity process an integral part of their management system. A customizable employee satisfaction survey can accomplish this assessment for your company efficiently and conveniently. It can help your management team determine which challenges and obstacles to diversity are present in your workplace and which policies need to be added or eliminated. Reassessment can then determine the success of you diversity in the workplace plan implementation.

Development of Diversity in the Workplace Plan: Choosing a survey provider that provides comprehensive reporting is a key decision. That report will be the beginning structure of your diversity in the workplace plan. The plan must be comprehensive, attainable and measurable. An organization must decide what changes need to be made and a timeline for that change to be attained.

Implementation of Diversity in the Workplace Plan: The personal commitment of executive and managerial teams is a must. Leaders and managers within organizations must incorporate diversity policies into every aspect of the organization's function and purpose. Attitudes toward diversity originate at the top and filter downwards. Management cooperation and participation is required to create a culture conducive to the success of your organization's plan.

Diversity in the Workplace Solutions Include:

Ward-off Change Resistance with Inclusion: Involve every employee possible in formulating and executing diversity initiatives in your workplace.

Foster an Attitude of Openness in Your Organization: Encourage employees to express their ideas and opinions and attribute a sense of equal value to all.

Promote Diversity in Leadership Positions: This practice provides visibility and realizes the benefits of diversity in the workplace.

Utilize Diversity Training: Use it as a tool to shape your diversity policy.

Launch a Customizable Employee Satisfaction Survey that Provides Comprehensive Reporting: Use the results to build and implement successful diversity in the workplace policies.

As the economy becomes increasingly global, our

workforce becomes increasingly diverse. Organizational success and competitiveness will depend on the ability to manage diversity in the workplace effectively. Evaluate your organization's diversity policies and plan for the future, starting today.

Conclusion

A diverse workforce is a reflection of a changing world and business. It helps to create a work environment in which employees of varied background feel welcome. In today's workplace every employee brings his or her unique self into the work place. It is important that this uniqueness is recognized accepted and valued by peers, leaders and subordinates, just as it is important for an employee to value the uniqueness of others too. These differences provide a range of skills and abilities that a team can tap to become a self-sufficient and successful. Managing diversity is more than simply acknowledging differences in people. It involves recognizing the value of differences, combating discrimination and promoting inclusiveness.

References

Choy, W.K.W. (2003), Globalization and Workforce Diversity: HRM Implications for Multinational Corporations in Singapore, Singapore Management Review, 29(2), 151-168.

Cox. T and Blakes (1991), Managing Cultural Diversity: Implications for Organizational Effectiveness, *The Executive*, 5(3), 45-56.

Kreitner, R. and Kincki, A. (1995), Organizational Behaviours, IRWIN Inc., pp. 55-78.

Robbins, R. (2011), *Organizational Behaviours Text Book*, Eleventh Editions, 17, pp. 32-36.

Thomas, R.R. (1995), A Diversity Framework, in Martin M. Chemers, Stuart Oskama and Markcostanzo (eds.), *Diversity in Organisations: New Perspectives for a Changing Workplace*, pp. 318-319, Sage Publications, Thousand Oaks, CA.

Kim Beeong Young (2006), Managing Workforce Diversity, *Journal of Human Resource in Hospitality and Tourism,* 5(2), pp. 69-90.

Jackson S.E. and Ruderman, M.N. (1995), *Diversity in Work Team: Research Paradigms for a Changing Workplace,* American Psychological Association.

15

Trade Unions in the Changing Economic Scenario

Birendra Nath Singh

Introduction

Trade unions in any country play a very crucial role in the growth and development of the country and as such Indian trade unions are no exception to this point of view. Traditionally, trade unions represent the interests of the working class and often conceived in real sense to be an agency to protect and project the demands and views of the working people against the repressive measures of the employers or the capitalists. But the contemporary views on trade unions broadly differ from that of the traditional views and thereby expect the trade unions to play a more positive role in the overall growth and development of any country like India.

India is well-known for adopting a balanced path of mixed economy (which is nothing but a balanced combination of capitalism and socialism) just immediately after obtaining its independence in the year 1947.

But with the advent of the economic liberalization process in India (during the years 1985-90), the role expectations of all the players of the developmental process, namely, the government, the employers and the employees (or say, the trade unions) have undergone a sea change to meet the challenges of the global competitions.

The trade unions as per the Trade Union Act, 1926 and in very simple terms are nothing but the associations of employees or workers for the protection of their rights and for the enhancements of their demands by capitalizing on their collective bargaining powers and use of their muscle and striking powers in case of actual confrontations. The employers on the other side are either the individuals or associations or forum of employers having enough money and muscle power to suppress or to deny the genuine demands of the working class or the trade unions as the case may be. Thus, there always a remains a situation of tug of war between the employers and the employees better represented by their unions. This creates an environment of confrontation and so called test of might by superior muscle powers.

And that might be one of the main reasons that although, India having so much huge stock of unskilled, skilled and highly skilled and technical trained manpower alongwith plenty of other human resources, it always remained lagging behind so many other developed and developing countries of the world in terms of productivity and quality of products and services.

According to available statistics, the productivity of the Japanese workers is on the average three times more than that of the Indian workers and the quality of their products and services is at least five times better than that of the Indian counterpart.

It is a known fact and matter of records that prior to World War II, the Japanese quality was considered to be the worst in the world. But Japan had the courage and the strong determinations to come out from this trap and stigma and since they decided to revamp their total quality and productivity policies so as to become a benchmark in these fields. They completed the whole journey from very bad and poor quality and productivity to be the world's best quality and productivity by adopting better people-oriented management styles. While in India, both employers and trade-unions went on waging wars against each other on all fronts without bothering even for a moment about their societal and national responsibilities and the impacts of these conflicts upon the future of the country particularly in an era of global competitions. This might be one of the main reasons, that even after enormous technological advancements, India still continued to be in the list of the developing countries of the world and the cherished dream of great leaders to be in the elite group of developed countries of the world remained unfulfilled.

According to available survey and estimates, India is the 2nd largest man powers in the world in terms of populations and also the 3rd technologically advanced country in the world. But then, the question comes that what has actually gone wrong with this country that it is still behind 100 developing countries of the world what to speak of joining the coveted list of the developed countries. The answer somewhere lies in the fact that it is nothing but too much presence of conflicts in various forms in general and trade-union related conflicts in particular as a result which about two lakh of mandays are lost every year in India. It is here that the government and other policymakers including the majority of the employers are compelled to re-think about the whole gamut of industrial relations scenario in the changed economic context.

Having heard the success story of Japan in terms of their participative and collaborative management styles, India also decided to implement the concept of labour participation in management and other related techniques like quality circles including "Works Committees" under the Industrial Disputes Act, 1947 in Central Government undertakings. The position of worker-director was also created mainly in the nationalized banks and other central government organizations. But this concept also ultimately failed in the field test barring one or two govt. or privates organizations, which were successful in implementing the labour participation in management concept in the true sense.

Some of the main reasons for the failure of the said concept are the followings:

1. Ideological reasons, i.e. class conflicts.
2. Mental barriers or different mindsets.

3. Too much politicalisation of the trade unions.
4. In-adequate educational qualifications/trainings and other competencies of the trade union leaders.
5. Lack of mutual trust and confidence on each other.

But this participative process also failed in most of the organizations, because of the reluctance of the trade-unions which had absolutely no belief in the participative process and rather they thought to enhance their collective bargaining and strike power to achieve their demands under the principles of pressure tactics usually followed by most of the trade unions.

But again, with the advent of the multinational companies setting up their plants in India and their corresponding demands for more congenial and harmonious industrial relation environments under which they may prefer to invest massively in India, the entire strategy had to be revised once again. As a consequence of this strategy, they mounted tremendous pressure on the Indian government to amend certain existing pro-trade union Acts like the Trade Union Act, 1926, the Industrial Disputes (I.D.) Act, 1947 etc. Moreover, they also demanded a counter-guarantee from the Government of India in respect their investments in India assuring a safe rate of return on their all investments in India.

The Indian government having already opened up its economy, once again came under heavy pressures to place the New Industrial Relations Bill on the floor of the parliament to amend some of the existing provisions of the Trade Unions Act, 1926 and the I.D. Act, 1947.

The followings are the proposed changes suggested under the new Industrial Relations Bill:

1. Only 10 percent (maximum) of the office bearers can be from outsider (i.e. 90 percent of the union office-bearers should be actual workers).
2. Minimum 10 percent (of the actual strength) memberships will be a must for getting registration (as against only seven members at present is sufficient to get the registration).

3. The memberships should be on actual basis and subject to verifications by the registrar of the trade unions.
4. The funds of the trade unions should not be used for any other purpose and never for political reasons.
5. There should be one and only one recognized trade union in one organization instead of the present multi-trade unions.

However, no political party in India was willing to clip off its trade-union organs and a result of which the proposed Industrial Relations Bill could not be placed on the floor of the parliament and naturally could not be passed till date.

Hence, there still remains a total stalemate in the matter, so far the multinational and foreign financial investments are concerned in India. This has virtually stalled the entire pace of progress and developments in India.

Hence, under the circumstances mentioned above, it has become very essential for all the players at the national level to formulate certain common foolproof strategies to cope up with the deteriorating industrial relations scenario having almost everyday either a bund or a go-slow or a strike. It really needs a more congenial and harmonious relationships at work places, so as to achieve the targeted outputs, productivity and international quality to survive the challenges thrown by the various multinational companies operating in India and abroad.

Suggestions

1. The proposed industrial relations bill has to be passed immediately on the floor of the parliament in the national interest by taking into confidence all political party leaders.
2. The trade unions have to come out of the "class-conflict ideology" and has to play a more positive and dynamic role towards achieving higher productivity and international level superior quality to make India great and vibrant.
3. The trade union leaders have to be adequately, technically

and professionally qualified and be competent enough to lead the working class effectively towards better goal.

4. There should be some professional courses both at under-graduate and also at post-graduate levels (with degrees and diplomas conferred by various institutes/universities) to attract and develop new generation young and dynamic trade union leaders in the country.

Conclusions

There is a proverb "never fight for having larger size of the cake, but always fight for enlarging the size of the cake itself, so that everybody automatically gets a larger size of the cake".

Building a nation is not the task of the government only, but is the task of all the segment representatives of the country, such as the government, the employers, the employees, the trade unions, the politicians and every individual, irrespective of caste, creed and religion with one and only one objective, that is to make India great.

There should be only one motto: nation is supreme. And if the nation grows, all of us automatically grow and are bound to derive the benefits of the total growth and prosperity of the country. It requires only the right will, the right vision and all out concerted efforts and that's all.

16

Occupational Safety: Evidence from India

Diptendu Simlai

Introduction

"Every twenty seconds of every working minute of every hour throughout the world, someone dies as a result of an industrial accident." This was how the seriousness of industrial accidents was described by the Director-General of British Council in his message of good wishes to the Seventh National Conference on Industrial Safety and Health organized by the National Safety Council, India. Thousands of employees throughout the world lose their fingers, eyes, limbs, and even their lives every day. Much blood flows in the sewers of industrial establishments. The hazard inherent in industrial work has made the life of the worker very uncertain. What is safety? In simple terms, safety means freedom from the occurrence of risk of injury or loss. Industrial safety or employee safety refers to the protection of workers from the danger of industrial accidents.

An accident-free plant enjoys certain benefits. Major ones are substantial savings in cost and increased productivity. Two types of direct costs are incurred by the management when an accident occurs. One is the compensation payable to the dependants of the victims if the accident is fatal; another is medical expense incurred in treating the worker if it is non-fatal. However, management can avoid such huge cost if the victim is insured under ESI or other insurance scheme, but the premium of such insurances is obviously a cost to the management. But, more serious than the direct cost are the indirect or hidden costs, which the management cannot avoid.

In fact, it is three to four times higher than the direct cost. It includes loss of account of downtime of operators, slowed-up production rate of other workers, material spoiled and labour for cleaning and damages to equipments. Therefore, a safe plant, by avoiding accidents eliminates these direct and indirect costs. Employees in safe plants can devote more time to improving the quality and quantity of their output. Therefore, to a large extent, safety promotes productivity.

Review of Existing Literature

It is a matter of great regret that occupational safety has been mostly a concern of the workers themselves and their trade unions and not of researchers so much. There has not been any in-depth research work on occupational safety in factories of West Bengal. Of course, we have survey reports like the Report of the National Labour Commission (1969), Report on the Survey of Labour Conditions in Rice-Milling Industry (1986), Report on the Working and Living Conditions of Workers in the Toys and Dolls Industry (1992), the Report on the Working and Living Conditions of Workers in the Readymade Garments Industry (1991), and the Report of the Second Labour Commission (2002). There was the Report of the Study Group on Wages, Incomes and Prices (1978). Much information is also available in Rudder Datt, *Economic Reforms, Labour and Employment* (2002).

We think that in our literature review we should give special attention to the Report of the Second National Labour Commission (2002), which focused very much on occupational safety at workplaces. The Commission recommended a general law related to hours of work, leave and work conditions in work places. For ensuring safety in different activities, one omnibus law might be enacted, providing for different rules and regulations on safety applicable to different activities.

The publications mentioned above reveal that many of the legal requirements in respect of workers' safety, health and hygiene inside factory premises, etc, are not being fulfilled in the majority of work places in India. But they do not give any special insight into the conditions prevailing in West Bengal. West Bengal is larger than many States of Europe and hence deserves separate study in its own right.

Objectives of the Study

As this study is related to safety of factories of different manufacturing industries, we have considered safety measures as described in the Indian Factories Act of 1948 and its subsequent amendments. In our study we have examined to what extent the factories surveyed by us have followed the provisions of that Act.

Industrial accidents are the end products of unsafe acts and unsafe conditions of work. There were 31,738 accidents (63 fatal) during the year 2004 in West Bengal. (Source: Government of West Bengal, "Labour in West Bengal") They usually occur as a result of the combination of a number of factors of which major ones are technical equipment, work environment and the worker. Most of the industrial accidents were caused by either unsafe actions or by unsafe physical work conditions or both and they could be prevented by correction of the unsafe acts and conditions. Proper steps always prevent or decrease the frequency of accidents. The safety design, installation, maintenance and operation of equipment and processes play a key role in maintaining a safe work environment. The Factories Act has provisions to maintain safe conditions of work up to a certain level. Strong trade unions can force unwilling management to undertake occupational health and safety measures.

The objective of this study is, therefore, to assess the actual safety measures taken in the manufacturing industries of West Bengal in the organized sector in the background of the Factories Act. In attaining our objective, we particularly wanted to know:

1. How far workers are satisfied with their present safety

measures?

2. To what extent management has implemented the safety provisions of the Factories Act, 1948?

We have taken up select factories in and around Kolkata (formerly Calcutta), one of the oldest industrial belts of West Bengal as well as India. Our survey area covered the districts of Kolkata, Howrah, Hooghly, 24 Parganas (North) and 24 Parganas (South), which contain the major portion of factory industry of the State of West Bengal.

Methodology and Sample

For preparing this paper, we collected a sample of 50 units from the industries, selected by us from different manufacturing sectors, on the basis of their importance in the industrial economy of West Bengal. We chose only the factory having at least 50 workers from the large industrial sectors. We prepared questionnaires giving the workers the opportunity of giving multiple-choice answers related to safety and collected answers from the concerned parties. Our period of survey was from January 2004 to December 2005.

After identifying the important manufacturing industries of the survey region, we divided them into 10 groups, in the manner of the Report on Annual Survey of Industries, Government of India. If we examine the above table it will be evident that not only the majority of the factories are situated in these 5 districts (survey region) of West Bengal, but also these districts represent majority of factory work force. Considering the total number of factories of each group in our 5 districts we divided the number 50 proportionately. We followed the cluster sampling method to find out the number of factories to be surveyed in each group of industries. In each group there are different types of industries also. Here, we did not follow any sampling technique. At least 1 factory was covered for each type. Finally, for selecting the target factory we followed the convenient method because our easy access to the factory and free conversation with workers was of utmost importance. 24 factories visited by us were ISO 14000 units. Every group of industry covered by us had both ISO and non-ISO units. Priority for a meet was given to the worker associated with a hazardous job.

We interviewed 10 workers from each factory. Thus, the total number of respondent workers was 500. The age groups and number of interviewed workers are shown in Table 16.1.

Table 16.1: Age Groups and Number of Workers Interviewed

(in years)

Up to 25	26-35	36-45	46-55	Above 55
100	100	100	100	100

Some of the questions, whose answers, because of their technical nature; could not be available from the workers, were included in the questionnaire for reply from the management. Where we found that the reply from workers contradicted the reply from management, we personally visited the concerned workplace to get an idea of the real state of things prevailing there. Thus, the survey findings have been derived from three sources: workers' statements made before us, management response to our questionnaire, and our personal visit and observation.

Sections 21 to 41 of the Factories Act, 1948 (amended) deal with safety. The safety provisions are absolute and obligatory and the occupier of every factory is bound to follow them.

Findings

Our research findings are shown below:

Fencing of Machinery: We found that most workers expressed the inadequacy in respect of fencing of machinery inside factories. The situation is most satisfactory in electricity and most unsatisfactory in leather according to workers. But we felt from our visits that the situation was worst in jute.

From the report "Labour in West Bengal" we observed that 33 percent of the total accidents in the factories in our state were due to machinery in the year 2004. Maximum accidents were placed in the jute industry (54 percent) mainly due to the old machines as per management view.

In respect of fencing of machinery, the ISO units were far better than the non-ISO ones, according to workers. Our actual survey finding was that the relatively new factories fare far better than old ones in both ISO and non-ISO units.

Machinery in Motion: As per the Act, machinery in motion must be examined by a trained adult male worker. The section further provides that any young person or a woman should not handle a machine, which is in motion.

In our survey it was discovered that the actual situation in respect of the above provision did not differ perceptibly from the actual stipulations of the act.

Young Persons Not to Work on Dangerous Machines: As per the Act, young persons are people in the age group of 14-18 years. Act says that young persons should not be allowed to work on dangerous machines.

We found that no young person actually worked in the factories visited by us. This was also confirmed by both workers and management.

However, we asked the workers that whether they operate machines within the risk zone or not.

Among the machine operators who operate the risky machine always, most of them are within the age of 36 to 55. That means neither young nor old do operate risky machines.

Striking Gear, Locking Device and Casting: These sections say that every machine must provide suitable striking gear. There should also be a locking device to prevent accidental starting of transmission machinery; no traversing part to be allowed to run within a distance of 45 centimetres from any fixed structure and casting should be done in such a way as to prevent accident.

In respect of the above provisions, the highly technical nature of the matter compelled us to rely upon concerned workers and management, and according to both the parties the situation is more or less satisfactory.

Restriction on Women and Children: As per the Act, women and children should be prohibited from going near cotton openers. We found that the above provision was followed everywhere.

Hoists and Lifts: According to the Act, hoists and lifts should be in good condition and should be examined once every 6 months. Similarly, lifting machines, chains, ropes and lifting tackles must be in good condition and should be examined once every 12 months.

Sound Construction: The Act requires that in every factory all floors, steps, stairs, passages and gangways shall be of sound construction and be properly maintained. Similarly, pits, sumps, openings in floors must be covered or fenced.

In respect of sound building construction the ISO units were far better than the non-ISO ones. Our actual survey finding was that the relatively new factories were far better than old ones in both ISO and non-ISO units.

Not to Carry Excess Weight: According to the Act, no person shall be employed in any factory to lift or carry excess weight which may cause his/her physical injury.

As per workers' response, in relation to lifting/carrying excess weight 16 percent of the total 500 workers still carry weight without trolley/machine.

In the ISO certified factories there was practically no manual carrying. Management informed us that in certain lines of production manual carrying was unavoidable for technical reasons.

Goggles or Screen: The Act mandates provision of goggles or screen to protect persons working on machines that might cause damage to his/her eyesight. We found that this provision was followed everywhere.

Not to Work in Gas Chamber: The Act prohibits entry of any worker into any chamber, tank, pit or pipe where fume is present, the Act also mandates that measures be taken to prevent explosion or ignition at gas or fume.

Our finding was that the above provisions were followed

almost everywhere as reported by management and also supported by senior workers.

Prevent Outbreak of Fire: Fire safety is important because it can save money and lives. The best fire safety practices prevent fires by reducing the chances of fire. Training workers in fire safety is a very cost effective way of preventing accidents from fire.

Regarding fire safety our question to the workers was "Is there any fire extinguisher arrangement in your organization?"

Our findings show that 96 percent of the respondent workers stated those fire extinguishers existed in their factories.

According to our survey, nearly 60 percent of these respondents said that the fire fitting system was satisfactory.

Our findings also reveal that according to workers the fire extinguisher arrangement of ISO 14001 factories is far better than in the non-ISO ones, also supported by our observation.

Most of the management of ISO factories expressed that fire prevention saves money by protecting property and lives, minimizes fire hazards and risks, ensures safer workplace environment, helps to show that the company cares about the welfare of its workers and may reduce insurance costs.

Safety Officer: If a factory employs 1,000 or more workers, there must be a qualified safety officer(s) appointed to ensure compliance of all the safety provisions.

Our finding is that safety officers have been appointed in all the factories having 1,000 or more workers.

Hazardous Processes: Because of the highly technical nature of the problem we did not consult the workers in the factories we visited. The management reply in all the factories was that provisions as per law had been made.

Results

Our own finding regarding safety, however, is that although these safety measures have been taken in all the factories where such measures are needed, most of the workers are indifferent in respect of these measures and thus remain accident-prone.

The management view is that safety measures are on the whole satisfactory. It, therefore, appears to us that accidents, when they occur, are not so much due to the fact that safety measures have not been taken at all or these are below standard.

The management view is that workers generally do not follow the safety regulations. According to them accidents are occurring mainly due to the negligence and/or ignorance of workers.

As per our findings, out of 500 workers 48 percent experienced accident in the past (last 20 years), of which only 04 percent faced major accidents.

We talked to 274 machine operators working within the risk zone (out of a total of 294 machine operators) and asked them whether they got any formal training in operating such machines in such workplaces.

It is clear that only 114 (68+46) of them were trained, 146 (74+72) operators got trained gradually while at work with their seniors. We wonder that 14 out of 274 operators had neither any training nor did they receive assistance from seniors. 10 out of those 14 workers operated such machine regularly. That means that 2 percent of workers may face accident any time.

Irrespective of his/her education level and training, the common tendency of a worker is to avoid all the norms of operation and adopt short routes to start/operate a machine. Even workers with vocational training have such an undesirable tendency.

In ISO units, majority of machine operators were trained by proper training programme where as in non-ISO units training by senior operators is a convention. Those 14 operators who had neither any training they received assistance from seniors were all from non-ISO factories

Lack of proper maintenance of machinery is also a cause

of accidents.

The majority of workers' opinion is that machines were not maintained on a regular basis in most factories. ISO units are far better in this respect but still have to improve.

Conclusions

From an examination of the survey findings, we arrive at the following conclusions.

The safety provisions in most of the factories, visited by us, are far from satisfactory, and therefore require immediate attention of the concerned authorities for their redress. We wonder if the inspectors perform their duties faithfully and competently.

A safe and healthy work environment is the basic right of every worker. While our rulers have put great importance upon industrialization, health and safety seems to have received a low priority. It is true that legislation exists to protect workers' safety. But this has not been properly implemented. To be meaningful and effective legislation should be reviewed and updated regularly as scientific knowledge develops. The guidelines of the International Labour Organization have to be kept in view in this connection.

The management of occupational safety and health at the level of the manufacturing units requires safety audit in West Bengal. There is no provision for compulsory safety audit in West Bengal, although it is a statutory requirement in many States in India (as for example, in Uttar Pradesh).

The overall methodology of safety audit will consist of the following stages:

1. Collection of preliminary information regarding manufacturing process and hazards etc. through a questionnaire prepared by auditor before undertaking actual field work.
2. Examination of documents pertaining to safety procedures/systems.
3. Discussion with key personnel at various levels.

4. Physical inspection of the plants.
5. Preparation of report with recommendations.

The scope of the audit will be to verify whether the planned and documented activities are performed in accordance with written procedures and to verify by examination and evaluation of objective evidence that appropriate elements of a safety management system have been developed, documented and implemented.

The report of such safety audit has to be sent to the Directorate of Factories. This will ensure that the recommendations of the auditor are complied with by the authorities through the issuance of directions/guidelines from time to time.

In many Asian countries like China, Indonesia, Japan, Korea, Malaysia, Singapore and Thailand, there are national level occupational safety and health management systems. But in India there is none at the national level. We think that such a system should be developed not only for West Bengal but also for the whole of India. The measures included there are generally from the model based on the ISO 14000 series.

References

Grimaldi, J.V. and Simonds R.H. (1991), *Safety Management*, Richard D. Irwin.

Government of India, *Report of the 2nd National Labour Commission, 2004*.

Government of West Bengal, *Labour In West Bengal, 2005*, Department of Labour.

Hammer, W.C. (1976), *Occupational Safety Management Engineering*, Prentice-Hall, Englewood.

Heinrich H.W. (1959), *Industrial Accident Prevention*, McGraw-Hill.

Hogstedt, C., *Work-related Accidents and Diseases in Sweden: Possibilities and Limitations for Global Estimates Based on Swedish Experience*, paper presented at the WHO/ILO Consultation on Health Impact assessment of Occupational and Environmental Risk, Geneva.

Sharma A. M. (1996), *Aspect of Social Welfare and Social Security*,

Himalaya Publishing House, Mumbai, Stan Allen and Neal Etchells, *Health and Safety Frequently Asked Questions.*
Stirling Smith, Occupational Safety and Health in India: an attempt to estimate the real number of work related deaths. www.raqsmediacollective.net/globalvillage/work/h38b.htm.
Vernon H.M. (1936), *Accidents and Their Prevention*, Cambridge University Press, 1936.

17

Corporate Social Responsibility (CSR) and HRM

Anupam Ghosh

Conventional CSR Issues

CSR has been interpreted in different ways by the business world for decades. CSR has also started the debate on morality in business activities. A good business policy with an ethical reference has more influence on business. (Siltaoja, 2006) Moreover, companies gain competitive advantage and also maximize profits when operating both in CSR and business arenas. (Marom, 2006) The broader the social role conception of a company, the better is their social reputation (Gossling and Vocht, 2007) and businesses those are reluctant to indulge in social responsibility will lose their social importance. (Krishnan, 1973) The work which a company does for profit maximization brings responsibility. This leads to reputation and helps the firm to maintain a superior level of performance over time. (Roberts and Dowling, 2002)

The responsibilities of business increase in countries where the Government fails to fulfil their functions and hence the mere profit maximization motive should be shifted. Also corporations have greater developmental responsibilities in poor countries. (Kolstad, 2007) Environmentally conscious managers have a sense of duty and try to help by sharing the burdens of society by incorporating green decisions. (Hussain, 1999) The theoretical basis of environmental CSR shows that it can attract 'green' customers and investors; pre-empts Government decisions. (Lyon and Maxwell, 2008) Firms having more integrated environment management systems are better economic performer. Moreover, combination of natural environment and management functions helps to improve the firm's market related benefits. (Wagner, 2007) However, CSR perceptions need to be in synchronization with globalization and also with local problematic issues.

Globalization has indeed made the world a "global village" but it has to be understood that the world is still not a homogeneous playground for the corporate. The perception is that, products and services would appeal across the world markets with the same enthusiasm. Now this needs a paradigm shift, as cultural worlds do exit within the so called "village".

Hence corporate social responsibility must incorporate a system in which cross-cultural divergence is comprehended and imbibed by the management. The more is the flexibility towards a society, the more is the understanding of their aspirations and the more is the sense of responsibility of the corporate towards them. The objective of this write-up is to reveal the thin line which segregates a citizen from a shareholder.

How is the citizen's role bigger than a mere shareholder; also if a business does a social service, does this make the manager a social servant. This brings us to another issue, who is the actual owner of a company—the shareholders or the society as a whole.

The crux of the discussion is to find out whether or not shareholder and the citizen share a common platform of trustworthy social responsiveness. Who is the real owner of a company? How is that the managers' agenda towards society somewhat matches with a 'civil servant'? Is it enough to interpret the codified law in a better way to enact social-welfare policies? Does political involvement of the managers solve the social awareness of the managers and Directors? All such presumptions melts down to the basic question that, in which way the company is oriented to the society? Corporate social responsibility is incomplete without intelligently surveying the cultural intricacies of society.

Some Reflections

In "A Shareholder, and A Citizen" Reich (1999), talks about shareholder as a citizen. As a responsible citizen his duty not to allow any corporate to cross limits of morality and ethical and social liability. For example, if a shareholder of a real estate company has to invest for a new project regarding building a resort in a slum area, then as a citizen he has to be aware of the viability and rehabilitation of the slum dwellers. He brings in an idea of control from the legislatures with more mutually acceptable laws, so that there is a symbiosis between the goals of the business and the social expectations. However, I say it this way which we need to balance between the roles of a shareholder and a citizen. A law abiding citizen cannot be so selfishly inclined to hamper the society both directly or indirectly for his benefits.

Law is for the society; so there cannot be double standards in defining it. Let's ponder why do agency problem arose? It is nothing but the mismanagement of the managers. So here shareholders lose the grip. However, if the citizen in him steps in, he can make or instruct the legislature (as a voter) to rectify such malfunctioning by enacting credible laws. So here shareholders, as owners, have a social responsibility of a citizen to make corporate a social entity. Now it's important to note that just being a citizen may not fulfil the social goals which the corporate wants to pursue. So, is it needed for him to act a bit like a social servant? Would the comparison between a shareholder (as an owner) and managers as a civil servant bring out the society's dominance over a business?

Now let us turn to what Dr. M. Friedman said in the article, "The Social Responsibility of Business is to Increase Its Profits". Friedman (1970), was talking about the managers would be a *civil servant* of they indulge in social responsible behaviour. The managers according to him cannot be both a public employee and a private employee, so he wants to leave the social work to the government. Here, the question arises—whether Friedman firmly used the word "civil servant" or not.

If he meant that managers having social responsibility would behave like "civil servants" then there are many questions left unanswered. Let us analyze:

1. He says that private employee or even a manager cannot be equated with a civil servant.
2. But all the private employees (or manager) are the agents of the shareholders. So shareholders are the principal (or owners) of a company.
3. On the other hand; civil servants are the representatives of those who select them (i.e. the government).
4. Government is formed by voting (in a democratic setup) by the public (i.e. society at large).
5. So the society is ultimately the principal and the civil servants the agents.
6. But society includes shareholders.
7. So society is the principal of the managers not the shareholders.
8. Hence, managers are bound to work according to the society, and be socially responsible.
9. Hereby, Friedman had nothing new to say, but rather contradicted himself and on the other hand agreed that business has social responsibility.

Here, we have to know that if the society is the real owner, then it has its own law which gives a direction to the business to run its functions. But sometimes laws have to be properly read and understood by the business people for being more social in reality.

In the article, "Corporate Directors and Social Responsibility: Ethics versus Shareholder Value", Rose (2007) said about codified law and focused on the helplessness of the directors trying to enact policies which are beneficial to the society, but ultimately failing to do so. He says that, though the directors may intend to be socially helpful but at the end of the day they have to follow the law; sometimes against their free-will. I think that this argument can be modified in another sense. Laws are made for and by the society, made for the well-being of all. So when the director gets the road-block from the codified law. This means their approach to a particular social responsibility is not in accordance with the law.

There is no use of accusing the law for being blind folded, it is the strategy that matters. May be that the directors have to revamp the policy to be in accordance with the law, keeping in mind the facets of social responsibility. This discussion can raise many questions like—does it only know the law necessary? Can the managers directly enter politics and start enacting laws (as legislatures) for their and society's benefit as a whole?

In the article, "Corporate Citizenship: How to Strengthen the Social Responsibility of Managers?" (Grit, 2004), the study brings up the concept of politicization of the management. He says, "Politicization is the most far reaching form of corporate citizenship, because it meets the wishes of mature and emancipated citizens or their representatives in councils, associations and movements." Here, I believe that politicization cannot be a realistic solution. As especially in countries with cultural diversity and multiparty system (e.g. India), the managers in this case if politicized would send a bad message for being biased and harbouring nepotism. On the flip-side the political leaders would try to influence vigorously and the corporation would lose sight of her goal and concentrate on intense lobbying. However, the managers should be politically aware of the trends and the voting patterns of a community or the country as a whole. This proves that mere politics is not a permanent solution for the managers to become more social than they are. They have to be a cultural being to get hold of the complexities and aspirations of different societies. This perhaps is the ultimate learning for the corporate to be socially responsible.

Another concept that seem to be very pertinent here is "Cultural Intelligence" which is somewhat defined as "an outsider's seemingly natural ability to interpret someone's unfamiliar and ambiguous gestures the way that person's compatriots would." (Christopher and Mosakowski, 2004) Here, the writers have tried to show that not only the managers should have the ability to show empathy to the people, but they should also be culturally intelligent to understand the pulse of the society.

This means that they want to make the managers come out of their little social shells and be magnanimous to accept other cultures.

Only being emotionally active is not enough, comprehending the culture is important too. It is only because we all belong to a socio-cultural background having different value system which may or may not be universally acceptable. To work with a group and to deliver to a community the managers need to follow their cultural setup.

This is perhaps the first step for the managers to become socially responsible because business cannot exist without active social participation. So in this era of globalization "cultural intelligence" is mandatory for effective and focused "corporate social responsibility".

In recent research, Moon (2002) emphasizes that the philanthropic CSR duties must be enlarged now to incorporate newer social issues.

CSR activities can be divided into three 'waves' or stages:

1. Community involvement.
2. Socially responsible production processes.
3. Socially responsible employee relations.

Conclusion

So it is quite evident that CSR cannot be just a strategy for philanthropic businesses. As CSR involves time, energy, money, foresight and human effort the expectations both within and outside the company also rises. This expectation can be in the form of human resource management orientation towards corporate citizenship, cultural intelligence and ethics.

The businesses need to understand that CSR comes from

the company functionaries itself; hence, CSR actually should be a part of HR operations. CSR is actually the employee responsibility of a company turned into social responsibility (with many added environments). So the society becomes a sort of extended family for the corporates. From the point of view of CSR, whether it is the case of directors following the law, or politicization, or citizenship, or being culturally aware, everything is a part of corporate strategy.

This corporate strategy has to extend itself from the traditional HR functions (such as compensation, training, development, recruitment and so on) by aligning such HR roles into sustainability initiatives. This strategy is nothing but the integration of social, environmental and profitability angles of a business which is needed for the long term survival of business.

Such integration requires lot of flexibility for the traditional HR functions; hence HRM becomes a dynamic process suddenly when it falls into the domain of CSR. This issue for HRM-CSR interaction needs much research in future; however one thing is clear that "CSR is dynamic HRM".

References

Christopher Early, P. and Mosakowski, E. (2004), Cultural Intelligence. *Harvard Business Review*, 139-146.

Friedman, M. (1970), The Social Responsibility of Business is to Increase its Profits. *New York Times Magazine*, 13th September, Reprinted in Beauchamp and Bowie 2001.

Go¨ssling, T. and Vocht, C. (2007), Social Role Conceptions and CSR Policy Success, *Journal of Business Ethics,* 74, 363-72.

Grit, K. (2004), Corporate Citizenship: How to Strengthen the Social Responsibility of Managers? *Journal of Business Ethics,* 53, 97-106.

Hussain, S. (1999), The Ethics of Going Green': The Corporate Social Responsibility debate, *Business Strategy and the Environment,* 8, 203-210.

Kolstad, I. (2007). Why Firms Should Not Always Maximise Profits, *Journal of Business Ethics,* 76, 137-145.

Krishnan, R. (1973), Business Philosophy and Executive

Responsibility, *The Academy of Management Journal,* 4, 658-669.

Lyon, T.P. and Maxwell, J. (2008), Corporate Social Responsibility and the Environment: A Theoretical Perspective, *Review of Environmental Economics and Policy,* 2(2), 240-260.

Marom, I.Y. (2006), Towards a Unified Theory of the CSP-CFP Link, *Journal of Business Ethics,* 67, 191-200.

Moon, J. (2002), *Corporate Social Responsibility: An Overview, International Directory of Corporate Philanthropy,* London: Europa.

Reich, R. (1999), A Shareholder, and a Citizen, *New York Times.*

Roberts, P.W. and Dowling, G.R. (2002), Corporate Reputation and Sustained Superior Financial Performance, *Strategic Management Journal,* 23 (12): 1077-1093.

Rose, J. (2007), Corporate Directors and Social Responsibility, *Journal of Business Ethics*, 73, 319-331.

Siltaoja, M.E. (2006), Value Priorities as Combining Care Factors between CSR and Reputation: A Qualitative Study, *Journal of Business Ethics,* 68, 91-111.

Wagner, M. (2007), Integration of Environment Management Managerial Functions of the Firm: Empirical Effects on the Drivers of the Economic Performance, *Long Range Planning,* 40, 611-628.

Index

Index